BORN
and
RAISED
to
HUSTLE

BORN and RAISED to HUSTLE

SEX AND DRUGS IN SAN FRANCISCO
DURING THE GOOD OLD DAYS

LEE DATRICE

iUniverse

BORN AND RAISED TO HUSTLE
SEX AND DRUGS IN SAN FRANCISCO
DURING THE GOOD OLD DAYS

Copyright © 2024 Lee Datrice.

All rights reserved. No part of this book may be used or reproduced by any means, graphic, electronic, or mechanical, including photocopying, recording, taping or by any information storage retrieval system without the written permission of the author except in the case of brief quotations embodied in critical articles and reviews.

iUniverse books may be ordered through booksellers or by contacting:

iUniverse
1663 Liberty Drive
Bloomington, IN 47403
www.iuniverse.com
844-349-9409

Because of the dynamic nature of the internet, any web addresses or links contained in this book may have changed since publication and may no longer be valid. The views expressed in this work are solely those of the author and do not necessarily reflect the views of the publisher, and the publisher hereby disclaims any responsibility for them.

Any people depicted in stock imagery provided by Getty Images are models, and such images are being used for illustrative purposes only. Certain stock imagery © Getty Images.

ISBN: 978-1-6632-4758-2 (sc)
ISBN: 978-1-6632-5833-5 (e)

Library of Congress Control Number: 2023922898

Print information available on the last page.

iUniverse rev. date: 02/07/2024

Contents

Introduction vii

Chapter 1	The Early Years 1
Chapter 2	The Booker T. Washington Hotel and Early Teenage Years........................... 13
Chapter 3	The Later Teenage Years, the Weed, and the Docks 43
Chapter 4	The Super Seventies 63
Chapter 5	The Family Side of the Seventies 77
Chapter 6	The Quiet Eighties..................................... 84
Chapter 7	The Limo Business..................................... 94
Chapter 8	The Present Day and My Foundation....... 116
Chapter 9	The Last Word 122

Introduction

When we talk about our personal history, many of us would like to think that our lives have been intriguing, unusual, sometimes funny, possibly varied, and potentially exciting. I'm sure the majority of your friends would agree with you about how absorbing your life has been. However, it is worth remembering that one of the reasons you're actually friends is that you have the same interests or share similar views. They will probably have lived a similar life or be into the same things as you, and thus your anecdotes will resonate with them.

It's when you start recounting moments from your life to absolute strangers and they tell you what an amazing life you have led, or what a fantastic ride you have been on, that you know your journey has been a truly fascinating one. That is what has happened to me. Time and time again, I have told people about some of the crazy moments from my life, going all the way back to when I was a young kid in the fifties, and every time the reply is the same: they tell me it is such a compelling story that I should write a book. Eventually, I decided to do exactly that, and you are now about to embark on the roller-coaster ride that is my life. It's a tale of San Francisco in the sixties and seventies during the city's heyday of sex and drugs, and of a man who was born to be a hustler.

When someone hears the word *hustler*, several different images come to mind. For some, it is the hustler in the pool halls, someone who makes money by beating the show-offs who think they have a genuine talent for the game. It's often enjoyable to watch them get dragged down a peg or two when an exceptional player hustles them for big money. Others will instantly think of the street hustlers, those with a plan to circumvent the rules to get what they want or achieve their needs simply through hustling people they meet. You don't have to be a bad person to get through life on the hustle.

Some people hustle just to get by, and those are the ones you should be cautious of as they genuinely need to do it; they will do whatever they have to because they need to survive. The opposite are the people who hustle because they can and not because they need to. I was six years old when my father first called me a hustler, and I continued throughout my life—because I could do it rather than because I had to do it. Some people called me a pimp or a drug dealer, but there was always far more to me than that.

For me, it was always about the hustle. My whole life, this whole story, is about me working hard, making my own money by working in day jobs, and everything else on the side. Even when I was selling weed, it would get too hot on the streets because they were busting everybody, but I didn't have to sell it as I was still working at the shipyards or in another more traditional job. I was never totally reliant on it. I had my job in the shipyards, and I would also sell weed there, and if I got laid off, I could work in the wrecking yards, and I could sell there as well. Whatever I did, I was after the money, and there was always a hustle. I am always on the hustle! I have always been ahead of things throughout my whole life because I get bored easily and want to do something different all the time.

I am lucky that I possess two polar opposite personalities thanks to my parents. My mother (and many in her part of the family) had that hustler side and that is where the hustler in me comes from, while my father and his family were all hard workers and that is where I get my strong work ethic from.

The way I am is a direct result of those two different types of people; I am both a hard worker and a hustler. This book is all about the wild times and the different hustles throughout my life, from selling weed as a kid through events involving my uncles and saving a policeman's life, to all the crazy moments running my own limo company. If you want to get an idea of the life I have led, then think of a Doc Holliday type—he was fast on the draw, and I had a love of Westerns as a child—but with a playboy-style attitude.

Almost everyone I have spoken to over the years has told me they wished they were me, and I sincerely hope that when you have finished reading this book, not only will you have enjoyed the stories, but you will also wish you were there too.

CHAPTER 1

The Early Years

Before I embark on the story of my life, I will tell you a little about my parents. My dad was considered financially well off, although as far as he was concerned, he was "broke as hell." My grandfather moved to Texas when his kids were little, and they bought a ranch where they had cattle and worked the fields. That is where my dad and everyone was raised, even though they were born in Opelousas, Louisiana.

Back then, when you had a ranch, you often worked somebody else's cattle, but you also had crops and suchlike that you developed. He had a bunch of boys and a few girls and that is how you did it in the South; you had a lot of kids in those days as you needed help on the ranch. My father stopped going to school in the third grade because he had to work on the ranch, and then his mother got sick and he had to take care of her. He was a bit of a mother's boy actually, as he spent all his time with his mom.

As I said, they had money, and my dad once told me that when he was around thirteen years old, my grandfather went to the general store and got his driver's license. In those days, there was no such thing as the department of motor vehicles and you didn't have to take a test; you just went up and got your license. While they were there, my grandfather said, "Get my boy one too." That was not the sort of thing you did if your family didn't have money behind them.

My mother was born and raised in Elton, Louisiana, and she came from a very big family, so big in fact that someone once told me that they had their own phone book because there were so many of them. My mother was really beautiful, and living in a colored neighborhood was always a good thing for her because all the guys were after her. That is why she eventually worked (and lived) at the Booker T. Washington Hotel.[1]

Unlike my father's family, my mother's side didn't have a profession or own anything like a farm; they simply tried to live a reasonable life and get by as best they could. They lived in this sort of colony-type place where they all worked together. If one person went fishing and got fish, everybody had fish. If someone went and got some pecans, everybody had pecans.

My father regularly went back to Louisiana and that is how my parents got together. The truth of how they became a couple is a little unusual for that time. My father originally

---

[1] "The Booker T. Washington Hotel: Harlem of the West," accessed on 8/30/2021, https://www.harlemofthewestsf.com/venues/the-booker-t-washington-hotel/.
Ben Zotto, "Looking for the Booker T," accessed on 8/30/2021, https://bzotto.medium.com/looking-for-the-booker-t-cb565824a691.

met and started dating my aunt, but when he went home with her one night, he saw my mom for the first time and was instantly attracted to her. My mother was younger than my aunt and an extremely beautiful lady. My father soon broke up with my aunt and started dating her sister, and the rest is history. In 1950, my father moved from Eunice to San Francisco looking for work. He was a welder and worked out of the foundries. He also told me he did shipyard work too, but didn't like to work at the docks because they laid off workers all the time. To him, layoff meant being fired, whereas to me when I worked in the shipyards, layoff meant vacation. He soon found work and went back in 1951 to get my mother. They were already together when he first came to San Francisco, and they got married in 1951, when he came back to get her.

My mother's family was quite poor, and they thought my dad was rich. When he married my mom, he even gave my grandmother a coal stove as a wedding present. In my parent's old wedding photos, you can see that my father got married in a nice black suit and he looked really sharp. I suppose you could say it was a type of tuxedo with gloves. My mom wore a lovely wedding gown. My parent's fine clothes were heavily contrasted by everyone around them because the rest of the people in their wedding pictures looked a little like hobos, which might sound harsh to some, but I want to be honest throughout this book. That was the type of town it was. Their hats were old and their clothes appeared to be khaki. (It was a black-and-white photo.) Back in Elton during the fifties, the combination of khaki trousers and a nice white shirt was considered well-dressed.

The Early San Francisco Years

They returned to San Francisco as a married couple and set about making a life for themselves.

I was born in 1952 and that is when it all started. I was their first and only child. My parents eventually broke up when I was six years old. My father went on to have more kids with another woman, but my mother never had any more children. During my early years, my mom slept a lot, so I just roamed around. I also started to cook for myself at an early age. Due to the late hours she worked, she was regularly asleep for long periods during the day, so when I got hungry and wanted something to eat, like bacon and eggs, I had to climb up on top of the stove and cook it for myself.

I started a fire on more than one occasion, but I soon learned how to cook. As a kid growing up in San Francisco, I was an only child and that did make a difference. I used to be that little kid who always wandered around the streets, like something from *The Little Rascals*. I started everything early, and at six years old, I began my first hustle, which involved pop bottles.

I wanted some candy one day, so I asked the lady next

door if she had any pop bottles. In those days, if you took your empties back to the store, you got five cents for the big bottles, three cents for the tall, skinny ones, and two cents for the little Coke bottles. She showed me her backyard. It was covered in fallen leaves, and she said, "You see that backyard? You clean it up and you can have all the bottles in the garage." It looked like they had never taken their bottles back to the store, because there was a whole load of them in that garage; it was more than a load, that garage was almost full of empty bottles!

It took me three days to clean her backyard and another three days just to get all the bottles out of her garage. I also cleaned up her garage as I went along, and I think that is where my strong work ethic first showed itself. I learned good work ethics and how to start a little business at the same time, all before I was seven years old. After I ate all the candy from that first venture, I wanted more, so I got my wagon and started to walk around the neighborhoods. I knocked on people's doors and asked them if they had any unwanted pop bottles. As I did that, I ran into other boys, and they said things like, "I don't have any pop bottles, but can I come with you?" I then asked them if they had their own wagon and more often than not they did, so I would tell them, "Bring your wagon and let's go." As we walked around the streets, we ran into girls, and they wanted to come along as well. We got them to run up the stairs and ask for the bottles as we stood below with our wagons. Before you knew it, I had my own crew of boys and girls, and yet I was only six years old.

At the end of the day, around four or five, all the parents were out looking for their kids, and they apparently kept running into each other as they tried to find us. You know how the conversation went: "Have you seen my son? No, have you seen my daughter? No." They must have driven or walked around several blocks as they looked for our group. There was a corner store about five blocks away and that is where they finally found us.

At that point, the parents turned up one after another, picked up their kids, and took them. Finally, my dad came to get me. It was quite late, and I was the last one to be picked up. He came down, looked at me, and said, "Boy, you is a hustler!" That was where my hustling career truly started, right there, with those pop bottles. When you have five to six kids and a large chunk of change is split evenly among them, you know that we were running a pretty good hustle.

My Family Roots

My pop-bottle venture didn't last long, because my parents broke up shortly after that (when I was still six years old), and I ended up going to Eunice with my dad because that is where he still had family and found his next job. In Eunice, he worked the fields and labored in other jobs like that, but he could not take care of me or watch over me, so he took me to his cousin's house.

They also had a working ranch, and it was all horses, cattle, and real cowboys; I loved that. I was born and raised in a city, and the only time I had seen a stable of horses was on television. I found myself right there with a real stable of horses, cattle on the range, chickens, and all sorts of stuff that I had only ever seen on TV. They kept me there for a while—about two to three months—but then school time came around and that is when I went to Louisiana to live with my mother's sister in Elton, and that was a big mistake!

Louisiana is full of snakes and alligators, so the whole time I was there, I had to run from snakes, alligators, and everything else you can imagine. I lived with my aunt for several months, and that is when I got into trouble for going down "the wrong side" of Louisiana. There were places in Elton where I wasn't supposed to go, because colored people were not allowed there. After all, white people lived in that area. I didn't know anything about this! I am actually light-skinned, but I was considered colored at the time. I even grew up in a colored neighborhood called the Fillmore District when I moved back to San Francisco.

There was this girl who lived up the road from my aunt's house, and she had this pony and cart. She would ride it all the way down from where she lived, turned the pony and cart around near our house, and went all the way back up the road. She often saw me as I watched her go up and down the road and made a point to turn around right in front of me. Finally, I decided to ask her if I could have a go myself, so I straight-up asked her, "Can I ride your pony and cart?" She replied, "Well, I don't know. Follow me up to the house, and I will ask my mother." When we got up there, she asked her mother if I could have a ride and she said, "Sure he can."

I was so happy as I rode this pony and cart down the country dirt road. The weather was perfect. It was springtime and our sour grass finally showed up after those miserable cold wet days that kept us cooped up. If you want to imagine it, think of *Seinfeld* and "The Pony Remark" episode. Every kid wants a pony and cart, especially if they previously lived in a city like San Francisco. I rode it down the road feeling the breeze all over my face and headed the same route as the little girl, toward my aunt's house and back.

Most of the time, I felt I was smarter than everyone else, which is the way I looked at it. The guy across the street had a dog, and she had some puppies. The dog was tall, skinny, and black, more like a cross of a Labrador than a particular breed. I asked the guy if I could have one of the puppies, and he told me that I could if I was able to get it from the dog. I then asked if I could take all of them, and again he told me that I could take all of them if I was able to get them away from the dog.

I told my cousin to run down to the end of the field to distract the dog. When she ran down to that end of the property after him, I took the puppies. When the guy came home at the end of the day, he couldn't find the puppies or his dog, because they were all at my house. The mother eventually came over to my aunt's place as she wanted to feed her puppies. Unfortunately, my aunt wouldn't let me keep any of them, as she didn't want dogs around her house, so she made me give them all back and that was the end of that.

I did have another pet after I gave the puppies back, but that sadly didn't end well. My uncle had a lot of hogs and one of them had some baby pigs. I adopted one of these little pigs and made him my pet. I looked after him, and every day I came home from school and fed him and played with him; I really looked after that pig. One day, I came home from school and I found my pig hung upside down with a bucket under his head to collect all the blood that had drained out. I asked my uncle, "What did you do to my pig?" and he replied, "Your pig?!" A couple of months later, we had some boudin sausages, and they were absolutely delicious. I tucked into them, and suddenly my uncle looked at me and said, "Your pig is good, huh boy?!" I never forgave him for that.

Even when my mother died and my aunt came out to San Francisco for the service, she said, "You still mad about everything that happened in Louisiana?" and I said, "You're absolutely right I am … Now get out of here. The sooner you leave, the better I will feel!"

Of course, I went to school in Elton. I attended the

Elton elementary school. A great memory of that school that I have is when I was in the first grade. The local fishermen found a sea turtle in the gulf while fishing for their daily job. It was so big they had to put a chain around its neck to hold it down. The fishermen wanted to show all the kids this huge sea turtle, which was as big as the car I have today. We all sat on top of it, and they took pictures of us as we all sat there on this huge turtle. I looked online to see if there might be any historical photos of that moment on the internet, but sadly my search turned up absolutely nothing. Once everyone had sat on the turtle and had their photo taken, there was a big turtle barbecue. Overall, that school was fairly decent and everybody was OK, as far as I was concerned. I don't have anything bad to say about my time there; it was just a nice, regular school.

My aunt went out and picked blackberries in the woods one afternoon. She loved to pick those big, juicy blackberries that you find in the wild. With a bucket tied around her waist, she picked the berries from the bushes with one hand and fought off the snakes with the other. After we ate those berries, I decided I wanted some more, so I went down to the woods to pick some for myself.

As I walked around and picked more berries, I came across this blue racer snake. As soon as he saw me, he stood upright, made this sort of whistling sound, and then he suddenly charged straight at me. I took off and as I ran, I changed direction from side to side rather than run in a straight line. I later found out that a blue racer can't turn easily. I don't know what told me to go sideways to get away from that snake, but I guess it must be in my blood. I ran, jumped up on the porch, and flew into the house.

I told my two aunts, who were both there at the time, that I had seen a snake and that it had chased me. I also told them I was sure I had seen more than one behind me as I ran home. My aunt went outside, caught one of them by the tail, and chopped its head off, but then she saw there was more than one for herself—a lot more in fact and it was all thanks to some local teenagers.

There was a wooded area with some grassland nearby and the teenagers had set it on fire. All the snakes had fled the area to get away from the blaze. My aunt and everyone else built a fire themselves. They would then grab any snake that came near them, kill it, and toss it in the fire. If they were too far from the fire, they threw the bodies over their shoulder and buried or burnt them later. There were so many that my uncle eventually let the hogs out, as did everyone else in town, and the hogs killed all the snakes that were left. At the end of the evening, they found all the hogs and put them back in their respective pens. I will never forget the sight of those snakes crawling all over the place.

It might have been a big mistake generally, but I cannot deny that my time in Elton was a good experience for me. I got to see where my blood—my mother, my father, and my family—actually came from. I also got to see a different side of life in the late fifties with the racial divides. In later years, my aunt often asked me, "When are you going to bring your girls to Louisiana and show them where they come from?" I told her, "They don't want to go to Louisiana, because they're scared to death of the place as I told them about all the snakes and alligators down there." She asked me why I said that to them and I told her, "I said it because it's true!" I reminded her that I knew this firsthand, especially when it came to snakes.

After that experience in Eunice and Elton, my father finally brought me back to San Francisco in 1959. He didn't stick around this time; he just returned me to my mother because I had been crying for her. He knew I wasn't happy and that I didn't want to live in Elton any longer. I wanted to go back to my real home, San Francisco, so my parents agreed it would be best if I lived with my mother. I am sure it was hard for him to send me to live with her, but he knew it was the right decision. That part of my life came to a close the day he dropped me off at my mother's place: the Booker T. Washington Hotel.

CHAPTER 2

The Booker T. Washington Hotel and Early Teenage Years

The Booker T. Washington Hotel was famous back in the day, but you might not be familiar with it even if you have lived in San Francisco for many years, because it was demolished in 1970 during a "slum clearance" redevelopment project. It was a six-story hotel with 125 rooms and was located off Fillmore Street. It was both a hotel and a nightclub and jazz lounge. It was the sort of place that had free radios in every room and television sets in each suite.

The building was originally known as the Edison Hotel, but it changed to the Booker T. Washington Hotel when it was reopened by William Bush in August 1951. A lot of famous musicians visited the Booker T. Hotel, whether it was just to rehearse or actually stay there. But the celebrities weren't just limited to musicians. During its time, the likes of Jackie Wilson, Little Richard, James Brown, Hank Ballard, Earl Grant, Duke Ellington's band members, the Nat King Cole Trio, Dinah Washington, Joe Louis, Willie "Stretch" Nelson, Archie Moore, and the Harlem Globetrotters all either stayed at the hotel or rehearsed there before they went off to play a show somewhere else in San Francisco.

It was well-known at the time, and the place is still fondly remembered by many to this day.

When you lived in and grew up around a hotel like that, people would always send you to the store to get them a pack of cigarettes, and that is how you made a little change. It was not unusual for the bartender to sometimes send me out to get a couple of bottles of alcohol. In those days, a kid could go to the liquor store to get cigarettes and alcohol because the people who worked there knew that they were not smoking those cigarettes or drinking that alcohol.

They also often knew you personally and knew who you were getting it for, so it wasn't a big deal if you went and got cigarettes for your mother. That hotel was where I met a lot of people who eventually had a massive influence on the direction of my life. My memories are full of people partying all the time and the bands and music. It was a time when things were very different. I hadn't realized how much I missed San Francisco and how many opportunities were provided to me. I was back on the hustle.

My mom was a waitress at the hotel and made a decent amount of money from that job. We actually lived at the Booker T. Washington Hotel, and she knew everybody in the area. When they mentioned me, they didn't use my name. They would say, "That's Arlene's boy," so everybody knew who I was as well. There was a restaurant around the corner that I regularly ate at and a car wash across the street owned by a guy named Sissy Brown. Sometimes he would watch me during the day for my mother and I would walk his dog.

There were all sorts of characters around the area back then. Sissy Brown was just one of them. He was quite famous to those of us who lived in the Fillmore District. He was a large man and maybe even the only homosexual like that around the city during that time; I don't know for sure, as I didn't know much about the gay scene in those days. He owned the car wash and gave me little jobs, like cleaning or sweeping up. He also regularly sent me to his house, where his mother lived too and paid me to take his boxer out for walks. I did lots of little jobs like that in my early years. He was eventually killed, and they found the bodies of Sissy Brown and his male partner in the trunk of a car. They were into drugs and probably involved with the mob, or so I heard anyway.

Some of the people I came across in my youth set me up for the varied and different things that I later experienced or got involved in. I met this working girl, Rita, and she was probably the best prostitute at the time down there, and she said things like, "This is my man," and gave me money all the time. She always took care of me, and I have always remembered her fondly for that. My early association with her eventually got me started on other things, but I was only seven years old at this point; I didn't know what to do or what it was all about at that age.

I took the money she gave me and hung out with her

son, but that was about it. Once we moved out of the Booker T. Hotel, I still went back all the time to see how she was doing, and I became well-known by all the hookers who worked down there because of that. Back then, hookers dressed up like movie stars. They all wore really nice clothes, and I suppose that is one way you could tell they were working girls: because they looked like movie stars as they walked the streets. I grew up around those hookers, and my love for women like that came about from the time I spent with them.

Around the corner was a restaurant where a lady called Lucille worked. She was one of my mother's friends and also my uncle's girlfriend. I often ate there as she always fed me when I was hungry. One night, we were all at the restaurant and the song "Green Onions" by Booker T. and the M.G.'s came on the jukebox.

Back in those days, they danced "real nasty." I watched my mom and everyone from behind the counter, and they all started dancing in that real nasty way. Suddenly, the police came in and took everyone off to jail. Honestly, they arrested everyone and took them off to jail just for dancing!

If you want to get an idea of the dancing I am talking about, this incident still reminds me of the Patrick Swayze movie *Dirty Dancing*. I remember they danced in a similar nasty and dirty way during that movie. I think it is safe to say my mom and her friends were not that good—remember that the people in the film were professionals—but they were certainly dirty dancing. Everyone had their own technique, and people in my day could all dance pretty well.

That film at least gives you a visual idea of how they danced that night. I walked back around the corner to the Booker T. Hotel, and the guy at the desk asked me, "Where is your mamma?" I pointed out the door and said, "She's in jail!" The memory that sticks in my head the most from that incident is of me pointing out the door and saying, "She's in jail!" I was just a little kid. I didn't know what to do. All I could do was walk around the corner and go back to the hotel. Suffice to say, we went and got her out of jail shortly after. The guy at the desk was another of my "protectors," because he knew my mother so well.

I had a bit of an attitude problem as a child, so my mom sent me to St. Dominic's Catholic School when I was about nine years old. As soon as any kid said something wrong to me or something that I didn't like, I immediately started a fight. My mom wanted to change that, so she thought that sending me to this Catholic school would help; it is safe to say that it didn't have the desired effect.

I recall an incident when people were protesting about things going on in San Francisco at the civic center. They had their placards and picket signs and were protesting about their rights and some of the decisions that were being made by the city politicians. Everyone felt the hippies were just out-of-work bums. They slept in Golden Gate Park and polluted all the areas they went to, and people felt they had too much influence on the laws and decisions that were being made about the city.

In hindsight, they changed the laws of San Francisco, and this somewhat contributed to making the city the way it is today. Nobody was on their side at all. These people were also unhappy with decisions that helped the rougher parts of the city—the places where I came from—and so there was plenty for them to protest about in their minds.

I was with a bunch of kids at the time. I don't know how old we were. I guess I must have been about twelve years old. One thing I do remember is that I was wearing jeans and a T-shirt, so I must have been pretty young. All these people were protesting around the civic center and city hall. The police had set up barricades to control the crowd, and we just stood near one of them as we watched and listened to the protest.

I said to one person, "You know what? If you don't like it the way it is, why don't you just leave? We happen to like things the way they are." A lady shouted at me. "You're a kid, what the hell do you know." I immediately started a fight with her and the other people who were around me. For some reason, and I am not really sure why to this day, the police just left us to it. I suppose they knew we were youngish kids of the city, and they just left us alone. It was many years later when I buried my mom at St. Dominic's Church—because it was her favorite church—where the nuns still knew me.

By this time, my dad had gone and got another job, and I saw him occasionally. He came back every so often because he knew that I was there with my mom at the hotel. He would come around and drink or party with people he knew. He tried to get back with my mother a few times, but it never worked out. We eventually moved to a bigger place because my mom only had a hotel room and we needed more room for me. Plus, it wasn't too far away so I could still go back. That is the place where I really grew up. It was on Ellis Street and down the road was a day-and-night place, and that is where the Rattlers motorcycle club (the Fresco Rattlers chapter) hung out.

My aunt married the head of the Rattlers motorcycle club, but he was just Uncle Jim to me. That was another part of my growing-up experience; I could do no wrong, because Uncle Jim would protect me or help me out. If I got into too much trouble, I could always run back to the Fillmore District. There was this one instance when we were chased by a bunch of guys in cars who were part of a car club. We had to run for our lives, and we ran straight toward the Rattlers. My uncle, who was this tall, skinny guy, stood up off his bike and then all his guys in the motorcycle club also stood up off their bikes.

The group chasing us in their cars had chains and swords, but my uncle and the Rattlers had more than that, so the car gang immediately swung around and took off in the opposite direction as quickly as possible. Uncle Jim and the motorcycle club were always there for me. If my friends and I got into a fight with a large group of people or a big gang and we suddenly found ourselves outnumbered or it became too many for us to fight, we could run back to the Fillmore District and it was like we had security.

That might sound a bit cowardly on the surface, but we were thirteen years old and often got into confrontations with late teens or even grown men. It was not unusual for us to hold our own in a fight against grown men, and just as we were about to get on top of them and finish things off, another load of men would show up. That is the point when it became too much for us, so we'd take off and seek help from the Fillmore District.

Back in the day, there were unwritten rules that you left women, mothers, and children alone, no matter what they had done, and that is meant more in connection with kids than mothers and women. You didn't mess with women or children. You often hear stories these days about men robbing or beating up women on the street, but it was not like that back in the sixties and seventies.

When I was a kid in the ghetto areas, the Fillmore District was like a haven. I was protected there. No one came into the Fillmore and messed with us because we were still children and the adults safeguarded us.

I had several protection routes in my early days—the hotel desk guy; Lucille, the working girl; or my Uncle Jim—and as I became a teenager, I even had the police on my side.

I had this basement when I was around nine years old, and someone broke in and stole my bicycles. We called the police, and they came out straightaway. Soon after, they had found every piece from all my bicycles stretched out far and wide across the area, in places like the projects and many other districts. They not only gave me back all the pieces, but they made the culprit's mothers pay for the damage. Every so often, for a decent length of time, somebody came over to our house with a check to pay for those bicycles. The police have always been good to me, even when things got a bit heavy. I don't know if there were many kids in San Francisco during the time I grew up who could honestly say anything good about the SF police department, but I never had any problem with them. In fact, all my life, they have almost always done right by me.

We dealt with problems differently back then. We used our fists to settle a dispute, and rarely did any confrontation involve guns. There were a few occasions that involved guns, of course there were, but not with the frequency they are used today. One of my best childhood friends and I always used to get physical with each other when we disagreed about something. It got so bad one time when I was about eleven that the neighbors called the police on us. They came out and said, "Hey, you, put your dukes up ... you, put your dukes up as well," and they made us fight it out. I was a heavyset kid, so my technique was to put you down on your back, get on top of you, and beat you up.

One of the officers worked out what I was going to do,

so he subtly grabbed my leg and flipped me over. My friend and I argued (in a less physical way) about it for years: how I would have knocked him out had the police officer not tripped my leg out from behind me. One day, out of the blue, it suddenly dawned on me that he'd done that to make it a draw, so we stayed good friends.

It might surprise you to know that I actually wanted to be a police officer for some of my childhood years. From about the age of eight until I was around eleven, I often hung out in the Golden Gate Park, where I played around in the trees and with my dog, and I regularly saw the policemen chase down criminals. The officer sometimes went after a criminal on foot, while the horse chased after a second one. The horse eventually jammed the perpetrator against a tree or wall and held him there until the officer came back. I thought that was one of the most amazing things I ever saw.

It was events like that in the park and elsewhere that made me seriously want to be a policeman (on horseback, of course). I wanted to have a horse and train him the same way, but that urge to be a horseback policeman also partly came from my love of a Western called *The Roy Rogers Show*, which was on TV during the fifties. However, I also wanted a police dog and that was because of another show on TV that I liked called *The Adventures of Rin Tin Tin*. That was also on television during the mid-to-late fifties, and they had a German Shepherd that helped the characters in the show.

My childhood dream was to combine the two; I wanted

to be a policeman with those two animals as my crime-fighting buddies but then I grew older and the sixties arrived—and so did the sex, drugs, and rock 'n' roll and that changed my whole life.

I stayed in school until I was sixteen, although I didn't graduate. When I was in high school—the Polytech High School—they had this mechanic shop and it was one of the best in the country. I loved to be in there and that is where a lot of my mechanic skills came from. For those who might not have had something like that at their place of education, it was a fully-fledged mechanic workshop with qualified instructors, and they knew absolutely everything there was to know about a car.

Someone told me that they got the idea for the mechanic shop scenes in the John Travolta movie *Grease* from my high school. The guy who told me that said, "Everybody I ever met who went to that school talks about nothing else but that mechanic shop!" This was a time when they had metal shops, auto-mechanic classes, arts and crafts, wood shops, and all sorts of practical classes and lessons. One time when I was at school, I suddenly felt hungry during a woodworking lesson and all I could think about was a T-bone steak. That inspired me to make a coffee table that looked like a T-bone steak. My mom kept that table for a very long time.

In my school years, either coming up as a teenager or during my actual teens, all we did was go to school and then at nighttime, we sometimes met up at the gym or played basketball. We often hung out in other places as well, and sometimes got into a bit of trouble—but nothing major. I still had my hustles during that period. I often cracked open parking meters and took the change, and I regularly stuffed cigarette packs up in the phone change slots. The way it worked was that I stuffed the open packet up where the change came out and all the change fell into the packet; I would go back later on and collect it.

As it was throughout my whole life, I also had more traditional ways of earning money. I had a paper route when I was about twelve in the Anza Vista district of San Francisco; it was a really nice area. I delivered newspapers each morning, and I always took my dog with me. It also gave me an excuse to be out early, when I could hit other neighborhoods with all my hustles and not look out of place.

At the same time, I also sold pills in the projects, on the 1st and 16th of the month when people got their paychecks or Social Security checks. This included pills like beanies, which was an upper that masked your hunger, and it was especially popular with the larger ladies; they often bought all I had. The "Red Devils" was also particularly popular in the projects, as was Tuinal, sometimes referred to as "Christmas trees" due to the coloring of the pill.

I recall this one particular customer when I was about thirteen. I delivered some weed to this guy, and his lady came out of the bedroom. She had this negligee on, and

I could see the red hair between her legs and her breasts were hanging out; my mouth hit the floor. The guy, her boyfriend, said to her, "Hey, honey, give him some honey. Give him some!" She took me into the back room and gave me some.

That is how it was back then. It was free love and no one cared about stuff like that in the midsixties. I obviously came back too often because the guy eventually told me, "You know, I don't mind you screwing my old lady, but you come around here too much!" After that, she came to my house instead. By the time I hit sixteen, I was involved with too many women, and she saw that I didn't need her any longer and stopped coming over.

To use a bit of slang from the time, she was a great piece of ass! My mother hated her, of course, as she didn't like an older woman coming over and taking advantage of her son. That would not be the first time she had an issue with me being with an older woman.

I had other jobs during my school years aside from being a paperboy. Around the age of thirteen, I left the paper route and started working at the Josephine D. Randall Museum. That only added to my love of animals, and it was partly responsible for my choice of monkeys, hawks, and snakes as pets. It was an after-school job, and I worked there for two years straight. I also worked at the San Francisco Zoo and the Fleishhacker Pool, where I was a junior lifeguard for the Red Cross. The pool was as big as a lake and was filled by the sea on a daily basis. They drained it out every night, and every morning refilled it with fresh seawater. Every day, several sand sharks made it into the pool through the screen, so before they closed the valve, we dived in and chased them back out. In the zoo, I hung around the pony rides because I always got to ride on them for free. That was my little adventure with the zoo and pool, and I worked there for a couple of years, albeit they were both summer jobs.

The fact I was a lifeguard meant I was in good physical shape. That is why I often told people, even in the hippie days, that the police couldn't catch me and that is why they came out with mopeds to keep up. However, they still couldn't catch me, because a moped can't jump a fence. Another thing that helped keep me fit was boxing.

At the age of thirteen, I went to Newman's Gym in the Tenderloin District. That was a really famous boxing place. I learned how to box, and I was pretty good as a boxer one-on-one; sadly, sometimes in the Fillmore District, it would be four or five people who would jump you, and it didn't matter how good you were as a boxer. I was even on the TV show *Wild World of Sports* one time. It was only a small clip; they were talking about the gym and my cousin, who was a boxer at that time, and I just happened to be with him that day. He was the reason I originally went down there and why I took up boxing.

They talked about the gym and his upcoming fight, and at one point they panned the camera around the room. As I saw it coming my way, I grabbed a kid and started punching him out to put on a show. The camera went on me for a brief moment and then switched back to my cousin. I don't know about fifteen minutes of fame. I think that was maybe my three seconds of fame. It literally passed over me in a couple of seconds.

The Tenderloin area was where all the speakeasies used to be, and it was a great place to go. There are a few theories as to why this part of the city is called the Tenderloin. One suggests it gained that name from a police captain who knew that his officers received regular bribes when they worked that beat and could eat well that night—they can afford to eat tenderloin steak tonight—thanks to the additional income.

There is another explanation along a similar line that claims the police got hazardous pay when they worked that difficult patch and again could afford to buy the best food. Other urban legends range from a reference to the soft underbelly of the city when it came to crime and criminal activities, and even part of a woman's anatomy, thanks to all the prostitutes who worked in the district.

When I was a kid, we spent a fair amount of time in the Tenderloin. We got into trouble, beat people up, and got into all sorts of crap; that's just how we were. One night, when I was in my teens (I guess maybe fifteen years old), I found myself in trouble with some people from that area and the police got involved. They stood behind me and then I suddenly took off to avoid any ramifications from the law, but they chased me and stayed on me longer than usual. I ran all the way through San Francisco, right to the far end, where the water is. I looked around and didn't know which way to go as there was nothing but water in front of me, so I turned around and ran back the other way. I guess the police eventually got tired or realized that I was not going to stop, so they gave up in the end. I simply walked home and avoided any serious trouble.

No matter what part-time or after-school work I was doing, I always had a hustle on the go and that was why I always had money to do other things with the marijuana and pills. I could always go and buy something and then sell it to make even more money. Back then, there was a place called the Playland[2] at the end of San Francisco. Playland at the Beach is another historic location in the city that no longer exists.

Its origins date back to the 19th century, but it became

---

[2] Takruri, Lubana. (n.d.) *Found San Francisco: Playland Historical Essay.* Accessed on 09/03/2021. https://www.foundsf.org/index.php?title=Playland

Takruri, Lubana. (07/03/2005) *San Francisco Chronicle: Insight Section: Playland* Original Source For The Above Page

Playland-At-The-Beach: OutsideLands.Org (n.d.). Accessed on 09/03/2021. https://www.outsidelands.org/playland.php

Winslow, M. (03/2014) *Playland At The Beach History.* Accessed on 09/03/2021. https://mksgrist.wixsite.com/playlandatthebeach/playland-history

Playland at the Beach in 1926. It had a roller coaster, a merry-go-round, a Ferris wheel, the Western-like "Fun-tier Town," a fun house, all sorts of concession stands, food stalls and restaurants, and pretty much everything you would have expected from a place like that. It was already somewhat on the decline when we hung out there in the early sixties, and it closed for good in 1972. Much like the Booker T. Washington Hotel, it was demolished and other buildings (like condos, in this instance) were erected on the site.

You can still find the odd remnant of the Playland in San Francisco to this very day. As soon as you walked into the original amusement park, you had Laffing Sal. She was always there laughing maniacally as you walked in, and as a kid, my dad had to drag me past her because I was scared to death; in my defense, I was a little kid at the time. She was a big animatronic woman who swung back and forth and laughed crazily. This was before my mom and dad had broken up. He would grab and hold onto me every time to get me past that insane woman.

Looking back, I suppose you could say I was a scared little kid in my early years. Once my dad won one of those big teddy bears, the type that was as big as a closet, and he quickly had to get rid of that thing. There was no way I would have stayed in the house with that damn bear in the closet! Don't get me wrong. I appreciated the gesture and that he had won me a "nice" bear, but I certainly didn't want one that was almost as big as him. As for Laffing Sal, unless things have changed recently, you can still see her in San Francisco today. She is located down on Fisherman's Wharf in the Musée Méchanique.

It might not look like it today, but Fisherman's Wharf used to be a decent place when I was younger. There wasn't much down there except the ships, and it used to be a nice place to drive around. Lots of people drove up and down the Embarcadero when the weather was nice, and most of them stopped at the wharf for some fish or crab. There used to be this guy with a stall who served fresh crab, and he cooked it while you stood and waited. Once it was cooked, he broke open the shell, pulled out the meat for you, and dropped it all into a container. It used to be such a beautiful scene with all the boats and the navy guys wandering around in their uniforms. It was truly a nice place to be, as opposed to the tourist nightmare it is these days.

We also had the roller-skating rink that I went to most Friday and Saturday nights. That was the most wonderful thing. I roller-skated, hung out with my friends, and danced with all the girls. Quite a lot of people used to go down there and that was a favorite hangout of mine. I sold my weed and pills down there as well. It was the perfect place if you wanted to skate and meet girls, but sometimes a fight broke out. There was always that one guy who skated really well. At this rink, Terry was his name. He was the type who always spun around in circles and performed clever, intricate dance moves. He always tried to show off and inevitably made a move on the girl I was with, and that was when I would whip off my skate and gave him a beatdown with it. While dancing with this pretty young girl I had, Terry started dancing circles around us showing off his dance skills. I turned my girl around, and Terry slid in and took over skating away with the girl. I was left standing there wondering what had happened. Once I saw them together dancing at the other end of the rink, I took my skates off and hit him in the head with my skate—knocked him out cold on the ground.

Another place I hung out, bought cigarettes real cheap, and found girls who wanted sex, was the Presidio[3] (This was when I was around fifteen or sixteen.) The Presidio was an old army base up by the Golden Gate Bridge, and of course, it was full of all those army brats and they were up for sex all day long. Their fathers were never around, and they all had emotional problems of one kind or another. It was a great place to get cigarettes and sex, but the Presidio also had a pool hall and a bowling alley.

I spent a lot of time up there. I played pool, went bowling, purchased cheap cigarettes, and chased those army brats around regularly. I had this one friend, who is sadly homeless today, and he dated this gorgeous girl who lived up

---

[3] *Presidio Of San Francisco:* Wiki2 (n.d.). Accessed on 09/06/2021. https://wiki2.org/en/Presidio_of_San_Francisco

in the Presidio. She looked like one of those beautiful movie stars, and he was so stupid.

However, the one downside to the Presidio was that it had its own police force, the military police, and other types of military guards. They checked me every time I came and went from the base. It was one of the few places where I couldn't sell any drugs, or very little if I managed to sneak some past the guards. In the end, that didn't matter a great deal to me because of the cheap cigarettes and the fact there was sex on tap. Those girls wanted it whenever I was on the base, and they always had a decent place to go where we could do it.

To be honest, it wasn't just the kids our age who wanted sex. The wives of the soldiers were also fair and willing game. Their husbands were off on duty and gone for a long time, and there was also the captain's wife and suchlike. I suppose that was partly to do with the Vietnam War as a lot of guys were away on tour.

The Pool Hustle

The Presidio was not the only place I played pool. Between the ages of fourteen and sixteen, I hung around with this pool shark. He was a hustler in the more traditionally expected form, and he could really play. We played at all the pool halls around the city, and sometimes farther afield. He taught me all I know about the game. In fact, any game I learned to play—be it checkers, dominoes, cards, pool, or whatever—I always learned from the sharks. If you could beat them in just one game, you could beat everybody else. That is how it worked; you played them and played them, over and over again, and by doing that you learned the game inside and out. Eventually, once you beat them, even if it was just once in a close game, you could beat anyone else. I often played checkers against the winos in the park, and in those days, you had winos and people like that all over the place, and they played checkers all the time. There was this one old guy called Whitey and no one could beat him, so I practiced with him all the time. It got to the point where I became so good that I finally beat him once and then nobody else could touch me after that; the downside was that nobody would play me after I beat Whitey.

It was exactly the same when it came to pool. I ran with Lenny, and our game plan was to practice over and over again. We bet a few quarters between us, and he always won all my money, but only just! Once he had taken all my money, albeit not a huge amount, somebody else would see him and say, "You want to play me? You got all the kid's money. Do you think you can beat me?" He was always honest. He would reply with comments like, "You see how good I am, right?"

They always wanted to play him despite the fact he had explained how good he was; however, the hustle was that they had not seen how good he really was! Once they swapped money a few times and that person started to put down some big bucks, he ran the table on them. He always shared some of his winnings with me as a thank you for my help to set up the hustle.

All of it—the hustle, the sharks, the seductive girls on skates, the games at the beach, the heavy smell of cigarette smoke and sweat, the various chitter-chatter from the customers floating in the backdrop—was what made the Fillmore District feel like freedom. And then there was the style. The guys all had hair fried, dyed, and laid to the side ... It was my home. It was where I grew up. It was my lifestyle. The guys all looked a bit like the Temptations; that is where I came from. We called it resting and dressing, although these days they have a saying called the mac: how a guy could talk the panties off a girl because he has the mac. That was supposed to have come from the Fillmore District.

Thanks to my lighter skin, I had these chat-up lines that I used when I tried to hook up with darker-skinned girls—things like, "Can a fella of my complexion go your direction" and that regularly knocked them off their feet. I had other lines like, "They call me the candy wrapper cause my wrapper is so sweet" and "once I love you, you won't love another." People told me that I was a smooth talker.

Around this time, you had those guys that sang together, a cappella, and they sang really well; they could have been somebody had they found themselves in the right place at the right time. You gave them some change and they bought a bottle of wine or something and then they all sat around and sang together. We just hung out next to them or around them and just listened to their music. Lots of girls walked by throughout the evening, and everyone tried to pick them up. I always stood at the bottom of the line, and if nobody else got them, I usually did!

Sometimes, I was so successful that I got their number and passed it to someone else at the end of the night as I had met another girl soon after. That was when I started to mess around with girls, at the age of thirteen or fourteen. We were all smooth and dressed nice—alligator shoes, double-knit slacks, flyaway shirts, and stuff like that—and that always caught the eyes of a girl.

It was at this point that I started to hang around with my uncle Herman, and back then he was the biggest dealer in San Francisco. Everyone called his crew the Jackals because they looked like jackals as they were all dope fiends. I began to dress in even better clothes because he gave me the money to do so, and I also got to drive his Coupe de Ville. He had this 1964 Coupe de Ville that was metal-flake green with a black top, and he gave me lots of errands to run that often meant I had to drive that car.

I suppose you could say that we were his little delivery boys, picking up packages and various other stuff for him, and he made sure he kept us dressed in really fine and decent clothes because of that. I regularly drove that car around the city, so it was inevitable that I got pulled over by the cops on a regular basis. The police knew him, of course, and that was probably another thing that kept me away from serious trouble with the law.

There was one time I was pulled over by the police that has always stuck with me. My cousin Alan and I were in that car and dressed sharp in leather coats, with our hair done really nicely because we processed our hair in those days; it was very straight with curls that came down the front. They pulled us over and asked, "Whose car is this?" I replied, "This car belongs to my uncle Herman," and all they said was, "Well, you tell Uncle Herman to have a good day!" That was it! We looked just like little rich kids. I could drive up to somewhere like the Fairmont Hotel in the Coupe de Ville with some girls in the car, and we were no more suspicious than any of the other rich kids at the time, so no one knew what to think of what we might eventually get up to.

As I look back at that time, I realize that was my opening for so many other things, especially women. That car, my clothes, and—somewhat—my money was when I started to get a lot of girls. Don't get me wrong. It was not like I had loads of cash, but I had lots of bling, as they call it today, and I regularly wore it. My uncle liked to go to the old San Francisco airport for a steak dinner. As we sat around with various girls and smoked weed at his place, he would suddenly just look around and say, "Let's go for a steak dinner." It was always a spur of the moment thing, and we'd jump in the car and go to the airport, watch the planes fly in and out, and have a quality steak dinner.

Everybody loved my uncle, including all my friends, and because he often took lots of different drugs, they would say, "Man, you have the coolest uncle in the world … that guy is so smooth." He talked like he floated on air because he was often high as a kite, but he wore a suit and tie, he had a nice car, and his hair was always perfect and all slicked back. Honestly, he looked like a white guy. If you saw him in the Fillmore district, he stuck out big time, like a sore thumb, but nobody messed with him because they all knew him. Anyone who didn't know him and saw him on the sidewalk probably thought he was the mayor or something because he stood out so much.

It was a little like something out of the film *A Bronx Tale*, albeit not exactly like that because the guy in that film was in with the mafia and dealt with the upper echelons of the organization, whereas my uncle was only at the top of his own thing. He was often down there in the Fillmore, and he certainly loved the colored ladies. One night, he paid a woman thirty thousand dollars just to sleep with him, and remember, that was back in the sixties! You might think thirty thousand dollars is a lot of money now, but it was an immense amount for that time. He always looked out for me and regularly told me to go to school, get educated—but get street smart too—and by doing that I would be doubly effective.

I suppose you could call this my gangster period. It was the time I hung around with my cousin Alan, which in hindsight, wasn't one of my wisest decisions. I almost got myself into some serious, life-changing trouble due to my involvement with his activities. I was about fifteen years old at the time, and I took part in a shop robbery with him and his regular crew.

We had just robbed this shop, and as we tried to get away, we suddenly found ourselves surrounded by the police. We had just stolen all the guns from this store, but as a mark of abject stupidity, we had not taken one single bullet. Maybe it was luck more than stupidity if you consider all the other potentially awful outcomes that could have happened if we had got into a shootout with the police.

At this point, we were in the middle of the Panhandle surrounded by cops, and they started shooting. None of us had any bullets, so I turned to my cousin and said, "Let's go, man," and he asked, "What about everybody else?" My response was pretty direct, even for me, "Man, forget these guys. Let's get the hell out of here right now. They are gonna come in here and take over. They have already started throwing tear gas and that's just the start. Let's get the hell out of here!" He refused to leave everyone else, so I asked which gun he wanted. He gave me a .38 or a 357 Magnum, and I said, "I'll see you when you get out." I grabbed a few guns and crawled out of there; I looked like a weasel on the ground as I crawled on my belly and slipped away.

Once I got out of the immediate area, I ran all the way home and that was not even remotely close. I ran as long and as hard as I could, stopped to catch my breath, and then ran some more. The whole situation didn't end well. Alan and his whole crew got arrested, and that was the problem. They got caught—of course they were going to get caught!—and his friends squealed on me because I used my common sense and ran. They didn't like me at all, so they ratted on me and that is when I moved to Brooklyn, New York.

New York Hustle

I was still fifteen when I went to live in Brooklyn with some of my other cousins because the police were looking for me. It was easier to do something like that back in those days if the heat got bad. There was no CCTV, no internet arrest warrants, or anything like that. I worked at a corner store, like a convenience store, and I stacked the shelves and helped people with their groceries. In return, they gave me pop bottles and a little change. I then got a job in downtown Manhattan as a walking delivery person. They gave me bus fare and money for stuff like that, but I walked every time and pocketed the extra money.

It was fantastic to be in downtown New York, and I walked every street in that well-known area thanks to the jobs I found. I had a role as a walking messenger, where you delivered packages to different buildings. I learned a little more about the city through that job. After that, I worked in a place that made elastic. That was also the time I went to "Boys High School," and that was a bit of a shock to the system. It was an all-boys school, and it seemed like there was a murder there almost every day. I suppose you could simply say that was just Brooklyn in the sixties (1968–69), and it was a tough area. The gangs in New York generally only controlled four blocks, so every four blocks it became like Louisiana with the alligators and snakes. Every four blocks I ran from one type of gang, and once I got four blocks over, I ran from another.

One night I was on my way home and saw this gang headed in my direction, so I crossed over and then they crossed over as well, so I crossed back over again and they did the same. I only had a Zippo on me, so when I got close to that gang and walked between them, I clicked open that Zippo lighter and it sounded like I had flicked open a switchblade.

The whole incident felt like it happened in slow motion. My idea to make the lighter sound like a knife must have worked as they left me alone and I continued, without incident, on my way. I would have jabbed them to death with that lighter if I had to because it was all I had on me to defend myself. Thankfully, it was enough to put them off, or at the very least it made them think twice about any idea they had to mug me. Sometimes, it paid off to be smart or think ahead and sometimes it was good to be just plain old lucky.

I suppose it helped during my time in New York that no one knew what to make of me. The city was quite segregated at the time, and all different types of people kept to certain parts; the colored people had their area, the Italians had the streets where they congregated, the Irish had their streets, and so on. I lived in a colored area, and no one knew what to make of me due to my complexion and the way I wore my hair.

Everyone in New York, no matter where I went, had a question mark on their face. It was like they were all asking themselves the same thing: Who or what the heck is he? Even if I told someone I was Black, they still had the same bemused look on their face because they could not put that together with the way I looked.

People have often told me, "Well, you don't look like you are colored." My daughter did one of those blood tests that tell you your heritage and mine came back with all sorts—I have some Irish in me, some African, and some French. My historical genetic makeup includes all sorts of things and that comes from my Louisiana heritage. That is why I am called Creole.

My mother was Creole and so was my father, though my mother was white Creole and my father Black Creole; either way, we are all Creoles. I think that confused so many people when I was in New York as no one could work out where I came from or where I belonged. I suppose you could argue it was somewhat the same in San Francisco, but there was no segregation involved there, so it was less prevalent or pertinent.

San Francisco Hustle Again

I spent about a semester in Brooklyn and returned to San Francisco in the summer of 1969. I came back to the city, and I immediately went to the judge and gave myself up. They were still looking for me, and I thought that it was the best course of action to end the situation. The judge asked me where I had been, and I told him, "Brooklyn, New York. I went to school in Brooklyn, at Boys High School." He asked, "You went to Brooklyn, New York, and you didn't get in any trouble at all?" I told him no, and he said, "Well, you must be cured. You come back here when you are eighteen and I will seal your record," and that was it. I still have no record today because of that.

I had learned a lot in my early days, or youth as it was in those days (presixteen), and much of it set me up for all the hustles and adventures that would follow in my adult life.

CHAPTER 3

The Later Teenage Years, the Weed, and the Docks

I suppose you could say that my adult working life started in 1969 when I was sixteen years old. My first job was at the docks in San Francisco and involved a multitude of different tasks. When I started, you paid ten dollars, joined the union, and could work for up to a month on the union card. It was a plug that you put in the boards, if you want to be specific. I started out on one task and then I came back and took on another because my ten-dollar card was still valid.

My first role involved these huge steel tanks in the shipyards. You had to go way down inside them, scrape the crusts off the inside, and clean them out. It was a bit scary at times as you had to go way down in there with nothing but a string of lights or something similar. However, it made me some money, and I was happy with that. I sometimes worked on the banana boats and occasionally found a banana snake in there. Everyone always took off in all different directions when that happened.

I also worked in the freezer section and that was a job where you worked two hours on and then two hours off because it was so cold. Another job involved loading coffee beans; you held a little hook in one hand, snagged it into the coffee bean sack, and then stacked them up. You loaded them up during the day and then they picked them all up and took them away. I was sixteen years old, and I worked alongside these grown men.

I stuck with the union that did all this type of work, and one of the main contracts they had (outside of work within the actual docks) involved cleaning up the bay. A couple of years later, in 1971, there was a big oil spill[4] where two tankers collided in the bay because of fog, and they hired lots of dockworkers and union members to clean up all the oil.

We did that by throwing some hay on it to soak up all the oil and then we used a pitchfork to haul the sticky mess back into the boat. We had to wear slicker suits, and it was hard and dirty work. However, I would say it was also pretty rewarding because once you saw the bay all clean again, you knew you had played a part.

To me, it didn't matter what the job of the day involved as long as I was able to make money from it. That is how I was able to buy my 1963 Lincoln Continental and start to dress in ever finer clothes. You also have to remember that

---

[4] "Tanker Collision Dumps a Huge Oil Spill in San Francisco Bay." (New York Times, January 19, 1971), accessed on 09/07/2021. https://www.nytimes.com/1971/01/19/archives/tanker-collision-dumps-a-huge-oil-spill-in-san-francisco-bay.html.

this work was not available all the time. It was an occasional thing, so I kept up my hustles throughout this period, be they existing ones or brand-new ventures.

This was also the time when I started to run into a whole plethora of different people from different places, like the merchant seamen. I guess they could point me out quickly because I was sat there with a big, old Afro and looking all fly due to the clothes that I wore—remember I was not a hippy, I was more like a hipster and wore things like long collars, nice shirts, and slacks with decent shoes. The weed side of my dock persona all started when someone threw a duffle bag of weed down and asked, "Hey, what can you do with this?" I smelt it and replied, "Shit, I can do a whole lot with this!" That is when I started dealing with the rich hippies and many other people that I have no intention of mentioning; all I will say is that you would know them if I named them.

That is when I started to sell weed on a bigger scale, and over time I was invited to all sorts of events because I had the best weed, the sexiest girls, and the finest cocaine. I moved around in a lot of different circles because of that. People invited me because they knew what I had to offer and who I was, either by reputation or because they actually knew me.

When goods came off the ships, they came from all over the world, and it was exactly the same when it came to marijuana with different types, like Maui Wowie, Panama Red, Acapulco Gold, and all manner of different strains.

Some came from Hawaii, some from South America, and some even came from Europe, and because I dealt with merchant seamen from all over the world, they passed my name around to each other, and thus I got more choice.

It obviously helped that I owned a car that someone could point out with ease, the Lincoln Continental. They always talked to each other and asked questions like, "Hey, man, I am hitting San Francisco next week (or maybe LA), do you know someone I could sell this to?" It was always my name that was suggested. Whoever recommended me then passed that person my phone number and told them to call me up. When they called me, we made arrangements to meet somewhere when they docked.

This guy called me up once and said, "I am going to be at the Los Angeles docks tomorrow and I got some marijuana. Do you want it?" I almost always said yes and asked them which dock they were going to be at, what was the name of the ship, all the information I needed to find them. I jumped in my Lincoln and took off, and when I got there the next morning, I had to be clever as they had security and checks. I innocently asked where a certain ship was going to be, and they simply told me.

I parked as near to that dock as possible and went to sleep because I had already told whoever I was meeting the color of my car and what I looked like. The next thing I knew, someone would knock on my window and ask for me by name. I gave him the money he wanted, threw the stuff in the trunk, and took off back to San Francisco. With my name being passed to all these different people, I ended up with contacts, suppliers, and merchant seamen who went all over the world. They picked up the weed (and other drugs sometimes) from one location and then they had this place at the front of the ship where they stuffed it and hid it so they could bring it all the way in.

My name got around to everyone, from one person to the next person, and the next thing I knew, I had calls from every different direction you could imagine. All they wanted was a chunk of money for their weed and that was good for them as they paid very little for it … if at all. They got a nice sum of money from me and then went about their business until the next time I saw them, while I, in turn, sold the weed onward and made more money for me.

My first connection with the longshoremen came when I worked at the docks. I reckon I first hooked up with them when I was about sixteen years old. I was on a break, and these guys came over and asked, "What kind of car you got?" I replied, "I got a Lincoln," and they immediately inquired, "That's got a big trunk, ain't it?" I confirmed that it did. They told me to back it up because they had stolen a pallet load of steaks and wanted to get rid of them, so they could quickly tear up the pallet and throw it away before anyone noticed it was gone.

I backed up, and they filled my trunk, a Lincoln trunk, full of steaks; you could not have squeezed another steak in there! I drove home with a trunk full of steaks, and when I got there, I ran up to my mother (as it was just me and my mom at the time) and told her to look in my trunk. "Where did you get all those steaks from?" she asked, and I told her, "The longshoremen gave them to me." The whole neighborhood had steaks that day. Everybody brought out their boxes and their bags. It was fantastic to live in this type of hood area because they always watched out for me to see what I might have got my hands on.

Hustle Woman

Girls were an easy catch for me, but pleasing my mom with my choice in women, not so easy. Throughout my life, I have had many different types of relationships with many different women. This was driven by sex, of course, especially in my younger years. But it was more than that. Around the same time, when I was sixteen, I was with this beautiful girl from Sweden. She was blonde with blue eyes, and she was built! She was about twenty-two years old, and my mother hated her guts. She always said things like, "That woman is too old for you," and I often replied, "I hear you, Mom, but you don't know all the good things she does for me." My mother was just funny about things like that. She always liked the women I didn't.

When I was seventeen, there was this light-skinned woman, and she looked like "our people" from Louisiana;

she was light-skinned, had really nice hair, and my mother loved her. I was far from keen because she already had a kid! The Swedish girl eventually worked on Broadway for me. She worked at a topless place and regularly got other work from well-off clients—she was kind of like a call girl in a way—and they paid her something like a thousand dollars just to go out with them on a cruise for the day. Sadly, she eventually left me for a lawyer, which is no surprise for someone as beautiful as she was.

Girls were an easy catch for me, especially girls from other countries, because of where I grew up and where I came from. A girl would come to America from Sweden, the United Kingdom, or anywhere outside the United States, and they would come to somewhere like San Francisco to see the lifestyle of the city: the sex, the drugs, and the music.

They soon ran into a guy like me and wanted to experience that kind of life, and I was able to give that to them because of where I grew up. They wanted to go down to the Fillmore District and one day be able to say they walked through that area. You have to remember this was not a place where everyone was welcome, and I used to walk through the Fillmore and people always asked me, "Man, where do you get all these girls from?"

I always looked a bit older than I was, so I got away with quite a lot when I was just sixteen. It helped that I used to have a little mustache and goatee. At that age, I used to go down to Reno, and they never asked me for ID thanks to the way I looked. I used to gamble on the tables, and on one particular occasion, I hit boxcars and that paid out something like twelve to one. I hit it six times in a row, and I promise you there was no hustle or anything going on, I just got super lucky. Unfortunately, when you got lucky like that in a casino, you drew attention to yourself and people started to ask questions. People started to crowd around me, and I decided to quit because it made me nervous; I didn't want to be asked for ID as I was too young to be gambling. I made a fair bit of money from the casinos over the years.

Hostess Hustle

After I started in the shipyards and began to make serious money with the drugs, I had the girls, the cars, the clothes, and all the things a young guy could ever want. That is when I had three different girls who worked with me, Pearline, Martha, and Judy. All three of these girls I met in high school, and they were all my girlfriends. That was the time when we went to or hosted our own parties and sold drugs—cocaine, weed, and pills—and that is when I started to meet the rich hippies. They were the people you could make some serious money from because they were really well-off financially.

You sometimes say someone has more money than sense, and I am sorry to say this was especially true of that crowd. They dressed and walked around the streets in kings' robes, and they had a lot of money. The women looked like queens, and the guys ran Cadillacs and Lincolns into the ground in six months simply because they could afford to then go out and buy a new one without worrying about the cost.

Most of these rich hippies lived down in the avenues by the beach, and sometimes I couldn't even tell them how much weed I had on me, because they would have bought the whole shipment that came into San Francisco. If I had three to six pounds of weed or something special that was really good, I told them I only had four pounds. It didn't work most of the time, because they still didn't believe me and said things like, "I know you got more on you somewhere." Of course, I had other friends and customers, including myself, and we wanted some of it as well.

I do have to give those hippies some credit because thanks to them not only did I make a lot of money selling drugs but I also gained from them in several other ways. For starters, I can say I have seen some of the biggest names in music from that time because they used to play in the panhandle for free. We all used to meet up there, smoke weed, and listen to music—bands like Santana, Jimi Hendrix, Janis Joplin, Jefferson Airplane, and, of course, the Grateful Dead. The concerts were free to watch, and before COVID, they still had some kind of show in the Golden Gate Park, but now you have to buy tickets and pay to get into the show. It's all very well trying to continue the tradition, but it's far from the same.

When I was younger, the rich hippies got together and

paid these people some money to come out and perform, so people got to watch them for free. Everything For Free was an actual movement during that time. That is why you found lots of places with their doors open, and you could go in there and sleep or have sex with any of the girls in there. It was a movement that they tried really hard to establish in San Francisco: sex, drugs, and rock 'n' roll, and all for free. It was this sort of thing that caused the aforementioned protests around the city when it first started up. These kids all came from rich families, and they traveled around the country with nothing but their thumb and a nickel in their pockets. Anytime they settled somewhere and needed thirty or forty thousand dollars to open a business or something of that ilk, they just wired Mom or Dad, who sent them the money, most of the time.

A whole swathe of them did exactly that; they settled in San Francisco and started different businesses like fish-and-chips shops. That was one of the reasons why the city is so synonymous with the Summer of Love in 1967. In the sixties and even the early seventies, you could go to one of those chip shops and get a roll of newspaper with steak fries in it for a quarter. For a dollar, you would get three big pieces of fish and the steak fries. They never tried to make any money from it, their main aim was to feed everybody and make sure everyone had access to food at a reasonable cost.

That is how all those clothing stores started on Haight Street, where you walked in, took off your jacket, and swapped it for another. If the new jacket you picked was better than the one you left, you paid a few dollars and took the new jacket home. It was a whole different world, regardless of whether you grew up in it at the time or looked back on it now many decades later. The hippies often wore the same clothes all the time; they were not dressed all superfly like I was or the people I hung around with.

The Everything for Free mentality stretched well beyond clothes, food, and music. These hippies would leave their cars up on Oak Street by the Golden Gate Park. They signed the pink slip, put it in the trunk, and left the keys under the seat or placed them in another hidden place, and while they were off traveling around the country, they told all their friends, "Hey, I have a blue 1961 Ford Fairlane parked on the side in Oak Street by the panhandle. You are free to use it when I am away. The pink slip is in the trunk and the keys are under the front seat." What they didn't know is that people like me had already found and taken the car. That was the car I got my driving license in when I was sixteen. I drove a 1961 Ford Fairlane and that was the car I used for a few weeks. We found a lot of cars going up and down that park. We found them unlocked, searched for the keys and pink slip, and then used it as we wished, sometimes for weeks on end.

I continued in the shipyards throughout this time. Sometimes it was just enough to carry my medical and things like that, but I was so busy with Pearline, Martha, and Judy and with the parties and the drugs. We were known as the best party hosts in the city.

Sometimes, somebody would call me up and wanted Pearline, Martha, and Judy to come over to the Fairmont, so we went to the hotel, got a suite up there, and then just hosted a party.

I had the girls and I had the drugs, and if I didn't have something you needed for a party, it was more than likely I could easily lay my hands on it. When you have got these big clients who have that kind of money—they just called you up and you just hosted the party—you could make so much money from it. They liked Pearline, Martha, and Judy being around, and aside from that trio, there were two other girls who I was associates with. These two girls were called Cookie and Brenda, and even though they weren't with me properly like the other three girls, they were my "most dangerous" girls and were always there if I needed backup. They always had my back, and sure, I could have sex with them if we all wanted, but we were not "together, together"; it was a relationship based more on being close and tight rather than something sexual. It also worked both ways as I had their back in return. They once got into trouble in Oakland, where a pimp shot them up with drugs, and I went over there and rescued them. It got a bit hot, let's leave it at that, but they would and already had done the same for me. When you deal with guys, they often want a piece of whatever you are involved in, but when someone cares about you, they will do it because of the way they feel about you.

My childhood sweetheart came back into town, and I invited her to work with me at these parties. I met Anna when I was thirteen in Los Angeles. I have a lot of family down in LA, so I went there quite often. She was a Cajun queen! She was beautiful, sexy, and so gorgeous that you could put her up on your mantel. She originally came from Hitchcock, Texas, and eventually came to San Francisco to be with me, but I had changed by that point. My outlook on life was different. I was on the hustle and didn't want her around my other girls.

I got her an apartment in San Francisco, in a nice neighborhood up on Bush Street, and we started to sell cocaine to support her. I soon became more or less just a drugs-related connection for her. She made enough money to pay for the apartment, buy the nice things she wanted, and generally live a decent life. She messed around and had other guys, and I didn't care, because I wasn't around all the time. I had her as my coke seller, and I just sort of supplied her, but she was also part of the entertainment with my group when I needed her.

When we had parties, and especially when we were the party hosts, I brought her along (because she had the coke) with my other girls. Everyone was happy with it and everyone had a good time, but at the same time, it was also about making money and everyone benefited from that as well.

In the days when I did parties, I would go and rent an apartment in a decent location, like Twin Peaks, and rent it for a certain amount of time, like a couple of weeks or a month. I preferred a place that was set back so you had a nice view that overlooked the city. I then added a few bits of furniture—a couch, a dining room table, and a bed—but that was it. I only rented it for longer periods, say a month, when I had a large quantity of coke I needed to get rid of, like a pound or something, and then I would arrange several coke parties to shift it as quickly as I could.

All these different guys came down to my parties. They bought their cocaine from me throughout the night and snorted it in huge quantities, and they also talked to the girls and tried their best to get them into the bedroom. Sometimes they succeeded and sometimes they didn't. Once again, remember, this was the time of free and easy love. Other girls also came along with the guys, and it would become a really fun party. People also brought drinks and some food and then everyone shared the booze and the food between them, and pretty much everyone snorted the coke. We sold the coke to everyone and anyone at the party, and we always sold as much as we could. Especially this one girl originally from LA. She sold her coke, and they were all over her like bees on honey. They all wanted her and tried to act like big shots. They would throw their money around like they were absolutely loaded, and this didn't influence her at all. These guys just spent and spent, and sometimes we ripped through that pound of coke in a couple of weeks. That was always a good thing because a lot of the time I owed people money for the drugs; more often than not, I paid half the money up-front but then I had to sell the drugs to pay for the other half. The next thing you knew, we were done with the coke, done with the apartment, and were gone.

In those days, you could easily rent a place with someone else's name. You didn't have to go through the sort of security checks you do in this day and digital age. Of course, the way I looked always helped; if you had an apartment to rent and I drove up in the Cadillac with a bunch of girls, you probably thought I was a playboy with some money. I would ask how much it was to rent your apartment for a certain amount of time, and you would tell me. I would throw down the cash and that would be it. It wasn't a big deal. I paid you for your time and your apartment and then you rented it to someone else when I was finished.

Credit Hustle

Credit cards were another hustle of mine, and I used to get them through the post office because I knew people working there (and they also sent me all kinds of other things as well). Once a new credit card would enter the post office, I could get it for a couple hundred bucks, and next thing, I would be in the department store maxing out the card or the service station buying tires as soon as possible, before they realized the card was "lost in the mail." Any name was on these fresh credit cards and only for a couple hundred bucks. It was easy activating these cards because they didn't have all the security aspects back in those days, like an activation code.

The girls and I used to go into shops all over San Francisco and buy all kinds of glamorous items with those cards. When I drove up in a Cadillac Eldorado dressed all nice with a car full of girls, they just figured I had lots of money. We used to go into the shops and buy jewelry, expensive clothes, fine perfume, the works. We used to shop in places like Macy's, and they waited on us like we were movie stars. They said it took a week for the purchases we made on those cards to show up, but I never took a chance and always used them for just three days. We used a card up to its limit. We did it in three days with the finest clothes, jewelry, and food, and then we got rid of it. We then did the same thing with the next card that came along.

The girls liked to go to nightclubs because back then there were these dance parties, and they always practiced their dancing. We went to clubs, and they got into dance battles with other girls. I just stood in the middle of them, and they danced the night away. I was not that much of a dancer, but they knew how to dance. If you want an idea of what I am talking about, you can watch the film *Soul Train*; they danced like they were in that movie. They loved all that because we were all young and knew how to have a great time. It looked good for me because I had three sexy girls, and they were either on my arms or danced around me. They often wore microminis, and the girls looked absolutely amazing when we went out to the clubs.

I do remember another story from my late teens—I must have been eighteen at the time—that involved my uncle and some color televisions. This one time someone drove up to me in this semitruck, and they came to me because they knew I had money as I was always in paid work. They had this semi full of color TVs and not many people at that time had one. They wanted a price for them that was well above what I had available, so I told them, "I ain't got that kind of money. Why don't you go to my uncle and see if he can do that." I called him up, and he said, "Yes, bring them down." As soon as I walked in, he handed me five hundred dollars and told me to go home.

The next time I saw these guys—it must have been a couple of days later—they said, "Don't ever take us to your uncle again," and I asked why. They told me he'd thrown down something like two thousand dollars and a bag of dope on the table and said to them, "You all go home, don't get back in that truck, and you are free. You got a bag of dope and a couple thousand dollars. If you get back in that truck, you're gonna end up in jail and it's all a waste!" They complained big time, but he told them to take it or leave it. He was tough to deal with, but everybody in the Fillmore had color TVs because of that. My uncle either gave them away to people who could not afford a set at all or he sold them as cheaply as he could so that as many people as possible in the area had a color TV. That was the sort of guy he was.

Color TV Hustle

My aunt recently reminded me about an incident when I was about eighteen or nineteen that involved my cousin Jimmy. He was a football player at Saint Mary's College, and he even became a pro! One day he needed a ride from his high school to the Golden Gate Park polo fields, where they practiced. I had this Dodge Dart at the time, and it was modified to go fast. So there I was, this kind of hustler-like teenager from the Fillmore with my cousin Jimmy, and he later told me I even scared him a bit. I had my hawk, Tim, with me at the time, a red-tailed hawk I used to fly around and his cage had a trapdoor at the bottom, where I hid my drugs.

I wanted to show him how fast my car was, so we zoomed about in this Dodge on the way to the polo fields. He admitted it was the fastest car he had ever sat in. Suddenly, from out of nowhere, came flashing blue lights behind us, and the police pulled us over. He put his head in his hands and said to me, "Oh Lord, I know we're going to jail." He was a good kid who had never been in any sort of trouble in his whole life. His parents had sent him to a Catholic school, like me, but he came out with a decent record and grades. The police officer leaned down and asked, "What's in the cage?," and I replied, "Put your hand in there and find out!" My cousin shook his head in disbelief, and the first thing that apparently went through his mind was, "Oh my God, now I know we are going to jail!" In the end, the policeman let us go once he investigated what was in the cage, thankfully not too closely!

I never knew it at the time, but my cousin Jimmy liked me in many ways, although he was also a little jealous of me as well. He eventually went to college, studied hard, and played football, whereas I lived the high life out on the street and did everything I wanted when I wanted. There was one occasion—he was at Saint Mary's at the time—and he wanted me to go to a party at the college. To be honest, I never really wanted to go, but he begged me to come along and I eventually agreed. I think it was partly because he wanted everyone to see me and see how I dressed all superfly.

Of course, this was the time when I worked and partied with the three girls, so I took them with me. We went along, but I can't say I overly enjoyed it. I basically stood around and watched all these fools from the college while they behaved like absolute idiots. A bunch of the guys started mooning everyone. I told my cousin and the whole party heard me, "You know, where I come from, we'd put some lipstick on those boys and some high-heeled shoes, and we'd have them out on the streets working. I can't be here hanging around with these types of people. I gotta go." I think my cousin just wanted his friends to see the type of family he came from. Maybe it gave him a bit of street cred. He told me he understood when I left.

I also always tried to help people whenever I could, like my cousin Alan or my friend Frank, who ended up homeless. I was always after the money and never stood around doing nothing or wasting my time doing things that were not useful. I had my own apartment, nice cars, and decent clothes, and I always tried to make as much money as I possibly could; that was the way of my life.

CHAPTER 4

The Super Seventies

In my twenties, I was still in the business of selling drugs—the usual things like weed and cocaine. But it was a time when a lot of my friends came back from the Vietnam War and brought back all sorts of drugs with them—cocaine, angel dust, heroin, and everything you can imagine from that country. They brought it back to me and gave a lot of it to me for free because I took care of them when they were younger. One particular thing they gave me was China white; it was a drug similar to heroin. I don't know how much of that stuff they got, but they gave me a lot of it, and I had that available for a long time.

I didn't go over to the war myself, but I do remember when I drove past Berkeley during that time and everyone was involved in a huge protest against the war (among other things). There were a lot of girls around during that period, and I have to be honest and say I had a very good time. I used to think to myself when I drove through there, "Do these kids ever go to school? They are always out protesting." My buddies had it bad because when they came back from the war, people called them things like "baby killers" and all sorts of really awful names. It wasn't their fault. Most of them didn't ask to go over there and fight; they were drafted!

The Vietnam War was a senseless war if you ask me. Those people fought with no proper weapons, not the sort of modern equipment the U.S. soldiers had available, and most of the time all they had was an old rifle, a bayonet, or a machete. Sometimes they sent young kids and babies into camps to do the most terrible things. You know how most American people are ... "Ahh, it's a baby, oh, look at that, wait a minute ..." That baby or kid walked into the middle of the camp and then blew itself up and killed everybody. They fought like that and won the war.

There is a lot to say about the Vietnamese people because they simply would not give up! We should never have been there, and it was a senseless, pointless war. A lot of people got hurt and not just the wounds that came from guns, weapons, or traps; they also sprayed that orange stuff out there, and it made everyone sick. If you didn't get killed in battle, maimed in your own camp by bombs, or seriously ill from all that shit they sprayed, there were still other dangers all over the place.

One of my friends told me that numerous prostitutes over there stuck razor blades inside their vaginas so when you had sex with them, you got your dick all slashed up. I heard all sorts of horror stories from people I knew who went over there. A lot of guys never came back from that war, and a lot of the ones that did return were all sorts of messed up!

It even happened to one of my buddies who used to work for me when we were teenagers. We sold weed and pills together back in the day. He was a little guy and people picked on him, so I was sort of like his protection, for want of a better expression. When he came back from the marines, he had a boxed jaw and could go through a tank with no fear! He wanted to kill pretty much everyone and everything he saw. He looked at me one day and said, "I would kick your ass, but you have always been good to me. But you shouldn't have ditched my sister like that!" I did indeed dump his sister at one point, but that is how I originally met him, through his sister. I met his sister, I had his sister, and then I met him, and that is when we began to hang out together.

I gave him a little work here and there so he could make a few dollars. He was part of my crew; it was not a hands-on crew, but various members came around sometimes and helped me out. It didn't matter who it was. However, he then went to the marines; I tell you, he could run through a wall even though he was only a little guy, no more than five six or five seven, but he was hard as a rock. He often had bloodshot eyes and a bloodlust type of look in them.

I have nothing but respect for those marines, but I don't know if I ever would or could have been a marine myself. They change you into something different. Having said that, I also knew another guy—he was a Russian and was like that as well, a tank! He was in the army rather than the marines, so I guess it must be a military thing.

SFPD Lifesaver Hustle

Everything sort of lit up during my early twenties. I did whatever I wanted when I wanted, and that was the time I saved a policeman's life. It was at the start of the seventies and must have been either 1970 or 1971. I was on my way home and walking through the panhandle toward the parking lot behind the DMV (Department of Motor Vehicles) on Baker Street. (We only had one DMV in San Francisco.)

I had just spent the evening with my girlfriend, the lady who would eventually go on to become my wife, and as I walked home, I heard this scuffling sound behind the DMV. Being a curious person, I said to myself, "What the heck is going on over there?" I quietly crept around the corner of the building to have a look. Now, there is one really important thing that you have to remember when it comes to this incident and that is the time when it took place: the early seventies. You have to remember this was a time when the Black Panthers were on the move and Martin Luther King Jr. had been assassinated just a few years earlier, and all this made what I was about to do a very tough issue.

As I finally set eyes on what was happening, I saw a difficult scene that was about to end in one of two serious outcomes. There was a policeman on top of a colored guy, and the guy underneath almost had his fingers on a gun lying just to the side; he was maybe two inches away from it. I assumed the policeman had managed to get the gun from his holster and now it was on the ground. The guy was desperately reaching for it, his hands were just two inches or so from the handle, and the policeman was obviously equally desperate to hold on to him and stop him from reaching for that gun.

They both saw me, and the guy looked up at me—and remember, I was looking all fly in my decent clothes with a big old Afro—and he said to me, "Brother, give me the gun ... hey, brother ... give me the gun!" I didn't have to think twice about what to do, and that was the right thing. I went and stepped on the guy's hand and then picked up the gun and gave it to the policeman. That was the sticky part of that situation, given that it was the early seventies: the fact I handed the gun to a policeman while he was in a struggle with a colored man. I could say it was a tough call, due to the racial aspect, but sometimes good things can sit equally alongside bad things, or a good conclusion can come from a bad event.

I suppose you could say that saving a policeman's life gave me just a little leeway if I got into trouble with the law. If I got in a spot of bother with the police, got arrested or put in jail (and it was never anything serious, maybe I got picked up with some weed on me), I knew his name (although, sadly, I cannot remember it now) and I would say, "Do you know Officer So-And-So? Call him up and he will vouch for me." They often called him up and then came back to me and said, "Ah, you saved a policeman's life! You are one of us, so you are free to go." As I mentioned in earlier chapters, they never really bothered me, and when you consider that they had already let me off lightly with a few other things before the time I saved that policeman's life, nobody ever knew what to think about me.

I remember that incident with the policeman vividly to this very day, and even in the seventies, with a guy from my part of the city about to get a gun and shoot a police officer, there was no way I was going to let that happen. I will say it again; I have never had anything against the police, even when it came to my drug activities, and they never did anything to me. As for the people on the street, it was never common knowledge to them that I saved an officer's life. I just never got into any serious trouble; I was always in and out of jail pretty quickly if I got arrested.

Even in later years, in the eighties when I had to sell weed again—when work got slow in the shipyards or at the docks and I had my wife, kids, and everything else—they still let me go. I wish I had found out more about him. I wonder how he came along in life? Having saved his life that night, I would love to know how his life turned out.

Love of My Life: My Wife Hustle

A few years after that, during 1974, I got married at the age of twenty-two and that deserves a whole chapter to itself. I had been working as a longshoreman for about six years and was looking to be a pipe fitter/welder at Bethlehem Steel. I tried to initially go in as a welder because my dad was also a welder and I knew something about it, so I started to fill out applications for one of the dockyard companies. I still had a shipyard job at the time, but I wanted to get into this one particular firm because a lot of the Irish guys worked there; I knew if I could get in with the Irish crowd, there was a good chance I could get a lot work.

I filled out application after application but never received a response. Therefore, I eventually went down to the office to fill out another application in person, and I asked the lady at reception, "Do they ever read my applications?" She replied, "Yes, and they put them over there," to which she pointed at a table that was full of applications. I quickly said to her, "Tell them the whole room will be filled with applications because I am not going to stop applying."

They soon called me in and asked me things like, "Do you know how to read blueprints … do you know how to weld this and that?" I just said yes to everything because that is my way; I always backed myself to be able to do something when I had at least a basic knowledge of that task or job. They told me they were going to put me through a test, and they did exactly that. Once I had finished, they said, "We know what you know now …" and I asked, "What is that?" They quickly replied, "Nothing!" I told them, "Well, my dad knows all about it," and the reply was pretty swift. "Just because your dad knows it does not mean you know it." I had to think on my feet, and I honestly just said, "Shit, I thought it was inherited!"

I obviously made an impression because they thought I was all right. They told me they would send me to John O'Connell Technical High School as an apprentice where I could learn how to weld and read blueprints. Of course, that meant I could also work at the company on apprentice wages; at that age, apprentice wages paid me more regular-basis money than I had ever seen in my life. I was more than thankful for the opportunity. I went to John O'Connell—and I worked there too—and then I became a journeyman after a couple of years.

I still maintain I was somewhat set for that job. After all, I wanted to be a welder like my dad, although in hindsight it might not have been my best decision, as it turned out I didn't really like welding that much because you got burned too often. The first time I got burned while welding was with my dad practicing in the garage. I screamed and dropped the welding gun and my dad yelled at me to suck it up. I used to watch my dad weld and a piece of slag regularly jumped up onto his arm; it always burned and smoked, and yet he just left it right there, like nothing had happened. I occasionally knocked it off and whenever I did that he would just turn and shout at me, "Why did you do that. You messed me up. Just leave it right there!" I tried to explain that I did it because it was burning him, but he didn't care and always told me to just leave it.

The time I spent with my dad gave me just enough experience to know how to weld. That was the trick, that was the key. They could see I knew something. I just didn't know enough. I showed enough knowledge to prove that the test wasn't my first rodeo. That is why they gave me the chance. They saw that I knew something about welding. I am convinced that telling them my dad could weld and thus so could I was another reason they gave me the chance to be an apprentice. I am sure they thought I had real balls to come out with a comment like that.

One of the advantages I had from the way I got that job was that I came in through the front door. Normally, you went through a union and got hired; the company then employed you for three days, a week, a month, or maybe two months. However, I took a different route and came straight in. By doing it that way, I was hired as a proper employee.

Thanks to my time in the shipyard, I was already a member of the union as well! If you went in by the front door as an employee, you became an employee and then you had to join the union. I did it the other way around. That is why I ended up with a steady job, and when everyone else was being laid off, I was still there. I needed that money because I had started a family and had bills to pay. That is the time when I had a steady job in the shipyards or worked for several other companies at the docks as a pipe fitter.

The docks were sometimes used as a set for the television show *The Streets of San Francisco*, which ran from 1972 to

1977. We couldn't work when they filmed, so we often sat on the roof and watched them create the scenes. The one thing I'll always remember was how they set cars on fire. They had guys that set up gas lines inside the car so when they threw a torch, it burst into flames. That was the amazing thing about that type of scene. They had a car that was already burnt out and then they had a second car that looked exactly the same but in decent condition. When it came to the explosion or they needed a car that was on fire, they just switched them over. I was fascinated to see how they did it and then sometime later be able to see that finished scene in the show.

Hard Work Hustle

Even after I got married, had a steady job at the docks, and had somewhat settled down with a quieter life, the longshoremen still knew me. They would find where I worked and ask, "Do you know what's in that container down there?"

When the question came from a longshoreman, it was usually a lucrative one for me.

I was asked that very question by one of the longshoremen when I worked at the dockyards as a pipe fitter, and the reply that came from him was, "bottles of Johnny Walker Red." The longshoreman had the layout sketch, the manifest, and all the paperwork, so they knew exactly what container it was in. This was all before it got into the docks' main filing system. I still knew all the crane operators, and I got them to lower a forklift truck all the way down into the ship's hold. I opened up the container, took out one of the pallets of Johnny Walker Red, closed the container, and sealed it back up.

They had these lead-like seals that went around them, so I used this little torch to heat it up, loosen it, and put it back together after we removed the pallet. I then got the forklift out of the ship and put some chains on the pallet so it could be picked up. I had one operator lift the Johnny Walker pallet out of the ship and drop it way down toward the other end of the yard, as far as he could go.

When he couldn't go any farther, I had the second crane operator pick it up, and by this time I had tied a rope to it, and he then took the pallet way back to the very end of the shipyard and swung it over the fence. As he swung it back and forth, we grabbed the rope and pulled it over the fence and out of the shipyard. Once it was over the fence and we had hold of it, he lowered it down and then the longshoreman and I separated everything. I grabbed whatever was mine with a forklift and then came back into the yard as if nothing had happened.

I always gave everybody their share. You gave it to the people you needed to and who you needed to keep sweet, and they in turn would let you get away with pretty much whatever you wanted. It was a case of "you scratch my back and I'll scratch yours!" As for the others, whatever I did was fine as they played no actual part and had no idea about it either. When they came to do their count, they broke the seal and expected to see thirty pallets in there, but they only found twenty-nine. It was often a case of "somebody must have made a mistake because there are only twenty-nine in there, and the seal ain't broken …" and that was it.

It wasn't just the longshoremen who came to me with opportunities on the side. More often than not, the things I got involved in were set up by other people who knew me or my reputation. They knew I had physical items that would help them or that I had a connection with someone who could provide them with important information—for example, someone who worked in a bank or loan office. It would always be someone who knew what was going on in that building, what to do, and when to come in. Everyone knew back then that if you decided to hit a bank for thirty thousand, which they often had in the cash register, there were certain bundles of cash you couldn't touch. If the cashier pulled out those bundles, gave them to you, and you took them, they would often contain explosive dye packs that marked you and the money. If you knew exactly what to do when you went in there, thanks to inside information, then you knew how to get around things like that. It might be which packs of money to leave behind in a bank or the combination for a safe in a loan office. A couple of my "friends" asked me to help them one afternoon. Throughout my life, people always turned to me because I always had the tools, the cars, or the money. I was somewhat hesitant at first and that should have been a warning sign, but I eventually agreed to help and drive them where they needed to go. As far as I was aware, it was nothing more than that.

You had to be smart; you needed to know exactly what you were going to do and how you were going to do it. Most importantly, you had to make smart decisions about who you got involved with. I made a rare bad decision on that front when I worked at the docks and got myself involved with the wrong people. In fact, it was worse than that. I not only got involved with the wrong people but I also got involved with the wrong *stupid* people!

I drove them to the bank to "pick up their money," and we all got arrested because their actual intention was to rob the bank. They had absolutely no idea what they were doing. That is why it was such a bad idea. I should have known better. I should have listened to my gut instincts and not gotten involved with them from the start, and I should have shown at least a modicum of common sense and asked them exactly what they were doing. I honestly thought it was a legitimate request for me to give them a lift to the bank to withdraw some money.

I went to court while I was still employed at the dockyards, and I told the judge, "They asked me to drive them down there as they had to pick up some money. I didn't know they were going to rob the place!" My boss from the dockyard was at the back of the court during the whole hearing. The judge asked who he was, and I explained that he was my boss. He said, "All right, you are dismissed, and you can go." I think the judge was lenient because I had a job and showed remorse. As far as I was aware, all they were doing was going there to pick up some money, and when they got caught so did I because I was the driver. That was the last time I got involved in anything like that. You should always learn from your mistakes and that incident taught me a major lesson. I was in my late twenties and it could have cost me so much, including the family.

CHAPTER 5

The Family Side of the Seventies

I met my wife in the early part of the seventies. I was driving down the road and made a right onto Haight, and she was standing there with her friend. At the time, I had my big Afro and a 1961 Cadillac Eldorado convertible. As I turned the corner with my hair in the wind, I saw her take a little look, like a double take. I thought to myself, *Oh shit, I got to get this one!* because she was absolutely gorgeous.

To give you an idea, if you have ever seen the TV show *The Good Times*, then you know it features a character called Thelma and she was stunning; I always loved Thelma in that show and my wife looked very much like her back then. I flipped that corner, came back around, pulled up to where she stood, and told her to get in the car. She replied, "I can't, no. My mother wouldn't allow this, no. I can't." I responded quickly and said, "I will take care of your mother later. Now get in the car." She could see it in my eyes that if she got in that car, then it was all over.

She refused to get in, so I asked for her phone number, and she gave it to me. We talked regularly on the phone for a year or two and she wouldn't do anything, but she eventually gave in. Once she did, it all changed. She was a model and a dancer, and funny enough that was around the time that song came out: "Brick House" by the Commodores. My future wife had me hook, line, and sinker.

Back then, I had a flat with three bedrooms, and my mother had one of them in the back with my stepdad. I had the other two. My girls lived in one of the bedrooms, and I had the third one. As my girlfriend, my future wife regularly came over, and the first couple of times she asked, "Who are these girls?" I replied, "You can call them the maids right now." She was determined to get me away from those girls, and she eventually managed it. After about a year of living there, everything was still going on and my wife didn't like it: the girls, the drugs, the parties, everything.

My mother enjoyed these women's company because my mom would do womanly things together like fix their hair, or they would fix her hair, and they did all that girly stuff with makeup and clothes. If I am honest, I wish I had kept going that way as I feel, deep down inside, that it might have saved my mother's life. My mother would have probably lived longer if I had been there with her. Don't misunderstand me; I would not change my life when it comes to my four daughters for anything in the entire world, but I sometimes wonder if I could have changed a few decisions around them. I will forever feel that I should never have left my mother, that I should have stayed with her and taken care of her, but my wife wanted to get away from all the hookers and stuff that I had around all the time.

Everything changed when I got married. My friends asked me, "Why would you get married, man? All the women you got, the lifestyle you got, why would you ever get married?" I just told them, "Man, because I am in love!" I was having so much fun and my premarried days were the best time of my life as far as I am concerned. My dad thought it saved my life, but you can never truly know which way that could or would have gone. My mother even asked, "Why did you ever get married when you have a bunch of women and a good life already?" However, my mother thought I should have kept going the way that I was at the time. I think my mom liked the fast life that I had before I got married.

I used to sometimes tell my wife, especially when I got mad at her, "My mother didn't like you, and she likes everybody!"

My wife and I are still together to this day, but the main reason for that is my four daughters, who matter more to me than anything else. I came from a broken family and did not want my kids to experience the same thing.

At that point, we moved to Pacifica and that is when things started to fade away in my life. My daughters came in succession every two years starting in 1976, two years after we got married. We got married in 1974, and my first child was born in 1976, and then my next child arrived a couple of years after that. I kept trying to get that elusive son, but I never got one in the end. I worked hard to give them a nice life and a good education. They all went to a private Catholic school, and they all went on to college. They are now all living their own lives.

My eldest daughter went to UC Berkeley and got a good education, while another got a master's degree as a social worker. She works really hard. She does a lot of work in the hospice area with people who are terminally ill. My third daughter had a tennis scholarship at state college and graduated with a bachelor's in business administration. She works in real estate and got married. I got to have my first son-in-law, who made my daughter a happy housewife. My youngest daughter also went to college, and although she never graduated, she is really smart and can get any job she sets her mind to. At one point, she worked three jobs at the same time. They have all worked hard, made decent lives for themselves, and I am immensely proud of them. There are not enough superlatives in the world or a dictionary to fully describe how proud I am of my four girls.

Although I never had a son with my wife, I do have someone who is every bit a son to me, and he is equally important in my life, and that happened because I spent some time with his mother when I was younger. She is ten years younger than me, and I have known her since her late teens. She eventually had a child through a bad marriage that broke up. She wanted to be with me again around that time, but no matter how much she wanted me back in her life, it just couldn't happen.

I had my job in the shipyards; I had my wife and daughters; and I wasn't going to leave my wife and kids. She eventually got married again, a couple of times in fact, and the second one smoked crack and messed himself up. I then came back into her life briefly when her son was four years old and then again when he was seven; I have been with him ever since, and now he is eighteen.

I have to go over there and chastise him from time to time, act like I am going to kill him because he's a young adult. He wants to hang out and smoke a little weed. I want to beat him sometimes when he doesn't work hard to get his education. He knows about my four daughters and the lives they have made for themselves, and I want him to be like them.

Every now and then, I have to go over there and deal with him. I am his dad and he calls me that. When I need to, as there is only so much I can do given I am not his real father, I sometimes ask, "Do you want me to still be your father because if you don't, I can leave right now?" He always tells me that he wants me to still be his dad. When he gets out of hand, I can't really do anything, so I just throw that back on him. "I don't have to be your dad anymore. If you don't want me to be your dad, if you don't want to listen to me when I am trying to help you …" I get right into his heart and hope that is enough to get him to listen to the advice I give him.

He has a job now, and it is right across the street from

the house. I have to stay on top of him because of that. I know he still smokes weed and was late for work one time; I don't put up with that, because when you go to work, you work; you do the other crap later. When you work, you work hard, you stay serious, and devote yourself to your job—you earn that money. I am trying to get him to buy a used 1991 Camaro like the one Snoop Dogg had, and he needs to work to save enough money for that. Without working and saving money, he is never going to get that car. I am trying to show him how to go for it; if you want it, you can get it, but you have to go for it and work hard first. I know he is young, and I suppose, in some ways, it is harder for me to deal with a kid because I know and understand what he is feeling, but it is also easier because I have been hustling since I was six.

Making money is what I do; this has always been what I strive to achieve and this has always been my pace. I have always lived my life in a way that I can do whatever I want to do, and not just in my employment. Even with selling drugs, I can still do the party as well. If you are out there selling drugs, partying, and all that stuff, that is how you sell even more drugs. I could do all that together even while I was working in the shipyards.

Even though I had day jobs, like the shipyard work or my pipe fitter role at the docks, I still had my hustles; I was still into cargo tanks, booze, mopeds, or whatever the longshoreman led me to. I still made that money, bought nice cars, and had a good life, and I want the same for him. My daughters have the same work ethic and have made great lives for themselves. I hope he will eventually learn the same lessons … sooner rather than later if I have my way.

CHAPTER 6

The Quiet Eighties

The eighties turned out to be a fairly quiet decade for me in terms of being on the hustle. I had my family to support, so I gave up hustling for more stable, more consistent paying work whenever I could.

However, the shipyards began to slow down badly around the mideighties, so I went back on the streets in 1984 and started to sell weed again. I sold it in the projects, and the projects were obviously in a bad part of town, but that is where most people sold weed during the eighties. This was in the heart of the ghetto, the corner of Webster and McAllister, and that was where all the thugs hung out.

At first, the guys didn't know me, so they started to crowd around me and wanted to jump me because I took a lot of their business as I always had the best weed. Suddenly, a bunch of my neighborhood guys came out, they looked like those penitentiary type guys with big arms and tattoos, and they had clearly been in "the pen" for a while. They came over and immediately said, "Nah, man, you mess with him, you mess with us because he was here first." They soon realized they couldn't mess with me physically or steal my weed, so they sicced the police on me instead and grassed me up.

The police came out to give them their dues. They dealt with me quite fairly this time as well. They asked, "What are you doing out here selling weed?" I told them, "The shipyards have got slow. I have four daughters and private school fees to pay, man. I also got a house up in Pacifica, and I gotta make some money, man. You got these dudes out here making money from selling weed. I am going to make some as well." They soon found out who I was and that I had saved a policeman's life once so that reputation within the police force kind of helped everything I did as I went along. I swear to you this is the truth: they lit up one of my buds and said, "Dawg gone, where did you get this from?" I told them: "I get it from up north 'cause them guys can't go up there!"

The next thing I knew, they had taken me to the precinct at 850 Bryant and locked me up in jail as they still had to take me in (even for a short while), but it turned out the place was full of my old homies and people I knew from the street, people I had not seen in a long time. They came from a period when we all hustled hard on the streets. We had this kind of family reunion. We kicked back and I don't mind admitting it: we had a good old time.

We all talked about why we were in there, and there were the obvious reasons—like selling or carrying—but the biggest reason we probably stood out to the police was because of the way we dressed; we all looked great and superfly because we still dressed the same as we did back in the day. The whole jail sat around and listened to our stories about the things we used to get into and how we got away with them. Finally, one of the officers came along and told me that I was free to go. The first thought I had was, *Goddamn it, they kept all my shit*, so I went up to the guy behind the desk and asked him, "Hey, come on man. Give me my shit back, man. You all gonna smoke my stuff, so give it back." The guy picked up my trunk key and said, "I know I can find another ounce in your truck!" The first thought that went through my head was, *Oh shit, they have already been in my trunk and found the rest, so let me get the hell out of here!*

I went straight to my car, bagged up the weed in the trunk, and went back out on the street to sell again. The next thing I knew, the police passed me by in their car and waved at me, and that was their way of telling me they did indeed have my stuff from the glove box and they were going to enjoy it later.

Even my best friend at the time was scared to talk to me after I got pulled in, put behind bars in 850 Bryant, and then got out without any backlash. We grew up together, and he would say things like, "Man, I ain't talking to you. You hooked up with the police. I am staying away from you, man."

I continued to sell my twenty-dollar bags until I ran out of weed. I sold about a quarter of a pound of weed a day and made something like four-hundred dollars, and when

I ran out, I went home. I should have kept going instead of returning to a steady job, but the shipyards opened up for a while, and I took the work while it was there. That was the last time I sold drugs out on the streets.

Later, once we were in the new millennium, I gave up smoking weed myself because I didn't sell it anymore and didn't like to pay for it. Besides, everybody has crap weed these days, and you can't get the good stuff any longer. Weed is not the same as it used to be. Lots of it is grown with chemicals and in labs, whereas it used to be grown wild in the great outdoors and in different countries.

Throughout the eighties, everything wound down for me. From 1986 to the early nineties, there wasn't much going on, and I was somewhat more laid-back. When I was about thirteen years old, I got into breeding dogs. My first breed was a Norwegian elkhound. So during this free time, I continued with my dog kennels and bred many breeds. I still had my dog kennels, and I had a lot of cars I worked on, which I'd buy and sell during these times. Here and there, I did a bit of work in the wrecking yards, for free, so I could get free parts for my cars.

I have always bred dogs and trained them, and I devoted more time to them when my children were younger. I have had all sorts over the years, including a boxer, a Rottweiler, a Saint Bernard, Doberman pinschers, Great Dane, and my favorite breed, the German shepherd. These dogs were all special, and if you came into my house and were an undercover police officer, they told me straight away. They got all fuzzed up. I guess there must be a type of scent that a person gave out, or maybe it was their mannerisms.

There was this time during the early seventies when my buddy brought this guy over, and he said, "This guy needs three pounds of weed," and my dogs just stood to attention and started to quietly growl. I looked at them and said, "Nah, man, I gave it up. It is illegal to sell weed." He was like, "Really?!" I told him, "No, man, I ain't sellin' no more." He knew I had it and repeatedly tried to talk me into it, but I told him I was done with all that and that I had no intention of getting back into that business. They left and he went to his cousin's house over in Oakland; his cousin broke out the weed and then they all went to jail. When he got out, he came over to my house and asked me how I knew, and I explained, "Didn't you see my dogs? They were telling you that something was wrong."

German shepherds were always my favorite type of dog, and I bred and sold lots of them over the years. I once sold a pedigree-bred puppy for fifteen thousand dollars. I also bred Saint Bernards at one point, and they are lovely dogs. I had one that was absolutely beautiful, and he always caught the attention of all the girls. At one point, I lived around the corner from Alamo Square Park on Hayes Street, and whenever I took him up to the park, all the girls ran over to him.

My German shepherds used to run up this big hill that

was behind our house in Pacifica, and they had chests that stuck way out as they were super fit from running up and down that hill. However, it was not wise to come around my house unexpectedly. A church member came to my house unannounced one time and ended up with forty-three stitches in his arm. He wasn't supposed to come around that day; we had seen him at church, and he had asked if he could pop over on Monday. In the end, he decided to come around that same day, and the dog chewed into him like chopped liver. She was a big German shepherd, and I raised her with my daughters. She was very protective of them.

Once the shipyard and dock work dried up, I turned my attention to other types of jobs to earn money. I even had my own delivery business for a while. I delivered newspapers in the early morning (*San Francisco Chronicle*), in the late morning I had magazines that I dumped at the doors in downtown San Francisco, and then I went up to the San Francisco airport for *USA Today* and dumped copies of that into the machines that dispensed them. In the afternoons, I had another paper route where I delivered the *San Francisco Examiner*. I made a lot of money doing all that. People couldn't believe how much I made through those jobs; I was like a machine.

I used to drive down the streets in my minivan—I had a 1987 Ford Aerostar—with both windows wound down, and I would throw the papers out from both sides as I drove along. I tossed hard, even the Sunday papers, and they were big and thick. I used to bag them and swing them over the top of my minivan all the way up to the top of that person's driveway. I even knocked paint off a few doors and had to pay for that. I broke a guy's grill one time as well.

My chest stuck out, my arms got big, and I could roll and throw papers like you had never seen. Even the police watched in amazement as I drove on the wrong side of the street and chucked papers left, right, and center—but it was three or four o'clock in the morning, so they let me get away with it. They even gave me a trophy at one point; it was an award for the Best Adult Newspaper Delivery Person because I could do more routes than anyone else. I had no complaints from any of my routes, and yet some delivery people got loads of complaints from just one. I had tricks, especially when I worked in an area where people stole newspapers. I often threw it over the car and hit the garage door so it landed right in front of the car. I even trained the people I delivered to. At first, I threw it near the car tire so when they came out and looked for their paper, they knew to look by the car tire. After that, I would throw it in front of the car where no one could see it and then the person knew that their paper would always be between the front of the car and the garage door. Some people just threw them at the edge of people's driveway and then other people simply walked past and took it.

I made over five thousand dollars a month from those jobs, but the best thing about them was the fact they gave me constant and steady work. I did that for six years straight, and I only had three days off during that period because it was an everyday thing, but it took care of my family. My wife will tell you today, regardless of all the other things she hated, that I always took care of the family. She never had to work. She stayed at home and took care of the children and the dogs: that was her job. I made the money and that was my job.

The eighties may have been a quiet and somewhat uneventful decade, but there was one event that deserves a mention. I suspect a lot of people will know about it regardless of where they come from and that is the Loma Prieta earthquake[5] that struck San Francisco on October 17th, 1989. That was the earthquake that caused parts of the Oakland Bay Bridge to collapse, where the top part dropped straight down on cars that were on the lower level. I had my house in Pacifica when the quake hit, the house where I raised my daughters for nineteen years, and it certainly shook, but there's also an interesting aspect to what happened locally on that day.

Across the street from us, there was a beautiful view of the ocean, and my wife wanted a house on that side because of that gorgeous ocean view. I wanted the place we eventually bought because it came with two big lots

---

[5] "San Francisco Earthquake of 1989: Britannica (n.d.)." Accessed on September 10, 2021. https://www.britannica.com/event/San-Francisco-earthquake-of-1989.

that I used for my cars and my kennels, and it's where my kids played. (They had a swing and a slide.) We argued and bickered about that and then the estate agent said, "You can put up a sea-view picture on the wall, and it's the same."

We ended up with the house on the opposite side of the sea view. In my defense, between the two houses across the street, you could still see the ocean! I built a table out there with a barbecue pit, and I often sat and looked at the ocean. To be honest, Pacifica is a very foggy area, so we only had six good days in the whole year.

When the earthquake hit, we were at home and the house shook a lot, but nothing major happened. However, the houses across the street, the ones with the ocean view my wife prized so highly, all those houses totally fell apart. Their structures all moved and that in turn wrecked the house. I suspect this was due to the fact they were nearer the cliff and their foundations were not as strong as those on our side, where it was flatter and sunken down with that big hill behind us.

Most people who were in the San Francisco area that day have different stories to tell, but sadly, a number of them are not happy accounts because over sixty people lost their lives that day. Some people refer to it as the "World Series Earthquake" as it happened right before the third game of the 1989 World Series between the San Francisco Giants and the Oakland Athletics.

That is really all there is to say about the eighties. I know that it's a time that many people treasure, a time when lots of things happened that they look back on fondly—be it the music, the culture, or even the fashion. Honestly, it escapes me to this day why people adore the fashion trends from the eighties and often talk of them coming back. Really?!

In the seventies we had great fashion, a few missteps maybe, but generally it was cool. If you take a look at the eighties, it was just crazy … bright neon things, Day-Glo stuff, leg warmers, shoulder pads in suits. I never got it and never will. As the eighties closed out, there were serious issues in San Francisco, but as I always did, I found a way to get through the hardship and bad times, make money, and keep the wheels of my life turning—on this occasion, quite literally!

CHAPTER 7

The Limo Business

With the late eighties being so slow, I had plenty of time to think. I saw a lot of people come to San Francisco and start their own limousine service. For some of them, I guess that was all they could do, and I started to think to myself, *I have got a Lincoln, maybe I should start a limo business of my own*, because a lot of those new drivers had no idea where they were going half the time. So I started my own limo business in 1991.

The biggest factor in my decision to start my own business was the situation at the shipyards and the docks. That sort of work became ever rarer and more intermittent, and I didn't want to remain a delivery guy for the rest of my working life. The Hunter's Point Yard was a naval repair yard until the midseventies and then it became more of a commercial shipyard until the navy briefly returned for a few years in the late eighties. At the close of that decade, the navy packed their bags and left for good.

To my mind, that is one of the biggest reasons why San Francisco became the nothing-much place that it is today. You have to include the army in that equation as well because the Presidio ceased to be a military placement around the same time in 1989. If you look way back through the history of the city, we always had the navy and that was the backbone of the nightclubs and all the things that happened out there. In years past, when you walked down the street, you always saw the crackerjack uniforms as the people in the navy strolled around the city.

When I was a little kid, my mother's cousin was in the navy, and when he came to visit, he often brought me a little navy outfit because I liked the look of it. I was a little kid then, but I really liked the uniform with the bell-bottoms, the shirt, and the cap. We often went down to Fisherman's Wharf and visited all the tours.

You only have to look at documentaries or films about World War II, and you will see that the majority of servicemen who came back from Pacific-based duty almost always came back to San Francisco.

We used to have a cannon at the front of the Presidio that looked out toward the Golden Gate Bridge, but everyone suddenly started to say things like, "Oooo, that is not acceptable. It makes it look like we are on a war footing. Something must be done about it!" In the end, they moved it all the way to the back so that no one could see it. These people are sick, and I am sorry to write that, but they are. People like me, people who grew up in the city and lived there most (or all) of our lives, the majority of us loved the Presidio. I don't know what happened to the world, I really don't—it just got crazy!

Once the navy left, the city went into a downturn. The navy had a big influence on San Francisco. If you look back, even in the early days, they used to go to places like the Tenderloin and kiss a girl for a quarter (or maybe a nickel) because they had been on the ships for a long time; they were called kissing booths. The guys could kiss a pretty girl and there was stuff like that just for the navy. There were also dancing halls scattered around the city where the sailors could spend their off-duty time or shore leave dancing the night away with girls. A lot of things around the city were there because of the navy. You could even say that the navy had a major hand in building the city into the place you see today, of course, following the Gold Rush from 1848 to 1855.

At the back end of the nineties, around 1996 to 1997, a lot of the city politicians talked about how they wanted to return San Francisco to its former glory, but that was never going to be possible because they had already got rid of all the military connections, regardless of whether it was the navy or the army. The military brought so much business to the city that it would be nigh on impossible to bring back the good old days to San Francisco without the sort of financial injection that comes from the military.

It doesn't help that present-day politicians and city officials do not have a cool bone in their body or any sort of swagger, so they have no idea how to make the city a hip place again, because they have no experience of what that means.

In fact, most politicians have no real-world experience, full stop. The vast majority of them have spent their whole lives in the political world; they study it at university, become an assistant to someone in politics, get promoted to higher levels through their early years, and eventually become a senator, mayor, or senior politician themselves.

You only have to look at the situation with the homeless. There are lots of ships around the bay area that are mothballed. Some have even been sitting there unused for so long that they now have plants growing on them. Some of these boats could house six hundred or more people; you could refit them with decent bedrooms, kitchens, medical facilities, entertainment rooms, and possibly even some workshops to help people learn skills or make stuff for the boat.

The sailors used to live for months at a time on these ships, and now they could be used to house our homeless. Instead, they just sit there doing nothing because the city officials have no foresight. It is truly depressing how the various political decisions from the early eighties to the end of the nineties ruined this great city. That is why it was absolutely clear to me at the start of the nineties that I needed a career change.

When the idea of a limo business first came to my mind, not only did I have a thought that maybe I could do it myself, but my brother-in-law was already involved in that type of work and told me how good it was, albeit he worked for somebody else. He was always dressed really smart, and my wife liked that part of it; you got dressed up every day, and back then you wore suits, a tie, and polished shoes, while some people even went as far as penguin suits. He worked for a company that was owned by an Iranian guy who had all this money, so he started to buy buses, limos, and all sorts of transportation. I wasn't that big when I started. I just had my own car, so I kind of worked for them as well, and did some jobs and bookings for them. That is what helped get me several of the jobs and contracts that I would later work on.

One of the biggest positives about my decision to start my own limo business was the fact my mother got to see me do it. She sadly passed away in 1992 from diabetes, and while I will always feel that I should have stayed around to look after her, I take a very small amount of comfort that she got to see me start my own business. That will always be a big regret of mine; I will always feel that I should never have left her. I always tried my best to take care of her, but as happens to most people, you get married, have kids, and move away to live your own life. My kids had a good life, so maybe everything happened the way it was supposed to.

Some people will tell you that their parents or grandparents always regretted that their children or grandchildren had to give up parts of their lives to look after them, so I guess there is regret regardless of the decision you make. Having seen all the things that I had done over the years, be they for better or worse, I will always be thankful she got to see this. As for my father, he passed away in 2011. He had a stroke and never recovered. I am glad he also got to see all that I achieved with my limo business.

I have always felt that I was a natural as a limo driver, for many reasons. First, I knew the streets of San Francisco exceptionally well, and I have also driven all over the state throughout the years doing other types of pickups, so I know California like the back of my hand. I also have a pretty good sense of which jobs to take, and more importantly, which jobs not to take! For instance, it often surprises people when I tell them that I did not work on New Year's Eve in 1999, the turn of the new millennium. I am sure that decision might seem rather odd when you think about the amount of money I could have made in just one night. However, I had a pretty good idea of what San Francisco was going to be like on December 31, 1999, and I didn't want any part of it.

I was told a few days later that it was a hell of a night in the city, but not if you were a limo driver. All the streets were packed and people walked on top of the limos to get across the road, and as the night wore on and midnight approached, they even jumped up and down on them; I doubt you need me to tell you that I would not have been impressed had that happened to any of my vehicles. Thankfully, I was not in the city that night, because I decided to go out for dinner with friends in Half Moon Bay.

You need both common sense and knowledge when you regularly drive something like a limo or bus in a city like

San Francisco, and I possess both. I know that many of the hills in San Francisco are too steep for me in a limo. If you attempt to drive up and over the wrong ones, I guarantee you will end up teeter-tottering at the top. There are plenty of other idiot drivers around the city who don't think (or probably don't even know) about this.

Spend enough time around San Francisco and you will see these amateurs drive slowly up one of the steep hills and then get stuck right on top, thus ending up like a seesaw. This even happened to someone during the time I worked with that company because one of their drivers got stuck at the summit of a hill in the city; if you look online, I am sure you can find plenty of pictures showing limos and buses stuck in this position around San Francisco, but I can assure you that none of them will be mine.

To be honest, I wish I had started the limo business earlier, say during the early eighties rather than the early nineties, because it was a great life. You often had guys coming into town and more often than not they wanted girls, so I linked up with the hookers again. I made a deal with them where I brought them the guys who wanted working girls, and they gave me a kickback in return; occasionally, I got a little myself as well.

I have always tried to stay ahead of the curve and be the first to offer something new or try something different if I thought it was a good idea that might lead to bigger and better opportunities. A prime example of this was my limo bus; I was the first person to have a limo bus in San Francisco, and maybe the first business to ever have one.

I went down to Florida and bought a small, old Greyhound bus and totally fitted it out with limo seats—bars between every two—two strip poles, lights on the top, mirrors all around the back on the inside, and a sound system. That bus became a huge hit in San Francisco in the midnineties. Once I'd taken it out on a few jobs and people saw that it was booked all the time, other businesses started to come up with ideas along a similar theme, but mine was first. These days, they spend thousands and thousands on these pimped-out extended limos, and I couldn't compete with that, but mine was the first and the original!

Turning my connections and relationships into profit and fun, I began to meet other girls aside from the "working girls," and one of those just happened to be a Raiderette. Personally, I am not a Las Vegas Raiders fan (or Oakland Raiders as they were at the time). I am a San Francisco 49ers fan, but when you spend your money with me, I can be a Raiders fan. For those unfamiliar with the term Raiderette, it was the name given to the cheerleading squad for the Raiders. We spoke to each other a few times, and one day some Raider's fans from Canada booked me to drive them around the Bay Area. They also wanted to go to a game.

I had my limo bus and asked the Raiderette if she would come along for the day, help entertain the guys, and get some money from it. Little did I know at the time but this would be the start of a whole business venture all on its own. I not only arranged for her to come along with us but I also organized a tailgate party for this group in the Oakland Raiders parking lot. I knew this guy, and he brought along his van, which had its own pullout firepit, like a barbecue pit, where he cooked things like burgers, hot dogs, and even lobster, and we also had kegs of beer and bottles of spirits on the go. At the time, I thought of it as a special one-off limo/catering joint venture for this particular group of Canadian clients. Given they were huge Raider fans, they absolutely loved my Raiderette friend and were all over her like bees on honey right from the start.

While we did the barbecue, she pulled me aside and suggested an idea that took our little tailgate party to the next level. She called over one of the guys with those little golf carts that you see around the stadium and disappeared off with him for around twenty minutes. She eventually came back with a little convoy of carts and with her were the rest of the Raiderettes, who she had invited to our party. We had to get the cart guys to stick around and act as security for us because everyone in the parking lot suddenly wanted to come and hang out with us. I had to constantly say things like, "This is a private party. You are going to have to go back over there where you came from!" Every time, without fail, the same response followed: "Oh, but I want to meet the Raiderette girls." I simply said, "I don't care if you want to meet the girls. Get your ass back over there!"

There was this one Raiderette, and she had those big fluffy lips. When she kissed you, they were so soft! As for the Canadian guys, they were practically on their knees as they fed the Raiderettes. We also fed the cart guys and made sure they were happy because they helped out and kept everyone safe from the throngs of people who tried to gate-crash our party. What was intended to be a one-off special occasion quickly became a semiregular event that my business offered. It became so big that I had to bring two barbecue guys, more food, and more beer because the client groups became ever bigger; it became a crazy event.

That is how everything starts; you do one thing and a few people tell someone else about it and then others want to do it as well. The next thing you know, you have three to four groups of customers who all want to pay to do the same thing. I paid my Raiderette friend a fee in the end, and it became a semiregular job for her. It also became a semiregular job for the guys I knew with the barbecue pits.

For a long while, all the parking attendants knew us and they all swooped around to help as they knew they would get a little money, some food, and have an enjoyable time. They knew the bus and knew they would get something for themselves when they helped out. Everything just clicked. Whenever the Raiderettes joined us, my Canadian customers (who became regulars) almost always started to throw hundred-dollar bills my way to thank me for arranging such an amazing party. Every year, they came down to the Bay Area and spent a lot of money with me, and I always made sure they had a great trip.

One day, my bus had a problem while they were with me. We were going back to the Huntington Hotel in Nob Hill, and while traveling there, my bus developed a wheel problem. I take the safety of my passengers very seriously, and I didn't feel it was safe for everyone to be on the bus with me, especially as we had to cross one of the bridges. Therefore, I said to them, "Look. I am having a problem with the bus. Something is wrong with the wheel, and I do not feel it's safe for me to drive you guys any farther. I am going to drop you off at this restaurant where all the Raider's fans go. It's barbecue and I'm sure you are going to like it. If you all stay there, I will go and get my other bus, and I will come back and pick you all up." They were quite happy with that, so I dropped them off at this barbecue restaurant and went to pick up the other bus.

When I returned to collect them, they were more than happy and told me, "This is the greatest place we have ever been. All the Raider's fans are here. We have got to come back here every time we visit the Bay Area. We love it!"

My Oakland Raiders connection extended beyond the cheerleaders. I had a bit of a connection with the Oakland Raiders in general because I used to drive some of the players to their surgeries. I had a contract with their doctor's office and drove them to and from their medical appointments.

There was this one player who told me about his

girlfriend and that he was pondering what he was going to do and where to settle down. I suggested to him that he should buy a house in Las Vegas—maybe I am clairvoyant given the team recently moved to Vegas!—and when he asked me why, I told him, "Because all the other Raiders have a house up in Vegas."

There was another player. I forget his name now. He and his wife came from Texas. He was a Dallas Cowboys fan at heart, but that does not affect who you play for. We used to talk all the time when he was in the car, and he even used to hire me separately from time to time as he knew I was a good driver. He once told me, "Since I have been in California, I have not had a decent one-on-one talk with anyone else bar you." I replied, "That is because I am real. I don't bullshit anyone." It was always a pleasure to work for him or his family.

Speaking of girls and limos, I regularly hooked up with the Budweiser Girls during the early days of my limo business. Thanks to driving them around during their heyday, every club in San Francisco knew me. When I drove up to one of the clubs or bars, say Johnny Love's on Broadway and Polk, Johnny would run out to my vehicle all excited and ask, "Have you got the Budweiser Girls with you tonight?" If I replied in the affirmative, he would quickly say, "Tell them to stay there. I want them to wear my T-shirts tonight." With that, he would sprint inside the club and bring back a set of his Johnny Love T-shirts, and the girls would pull off those little Budweiser tops that were tied in a knot at the front, with everyone looking on I might add. Everything was dangling out everywhere, and they would swap shirts for a short while.

When that happened, people often said to me, "It's fun to be a limo driver, huh?" and all I could reply with was, "Yeah, it sure is fun sometimes." Once the girls changed shirts, we all went into the club through the VIP entrance. That in turn became an advantage for my regular customers as well. If I picked up regular clients, Johnny Love would run out and ask about the Budweiser Girls, and when I told him that I only had my "guests" that night, he would still say, "No problem. VIP for your clients and I will charge you on the back end." It was something like ten dollars, and they got to go in through the VIP door and avoid the big entrance line that was always out front. These are the little things I can do for my customers that many other limo firms can't.

You get all sorts of passengers as a limo driver. One of the vehicles I used to drive had a hot tub in it. Unfortunately, they passed a law some years back that you couldn't fill it with water, because the limo was too heavy and it was hard to stop with a full hot tub. Therefore, we put a mattress, some silk sheets, and some decent pillows in it and turned it into this sort of nice bedroom. I had this one job where I had to pick up a client in Napa, and the customer simply wanted me to drive around for three hours. When I arrived at the pickup address, this lady came out. I have no wish to sound rude or unpleasant, but she must have weighed something like six hundred pounds. She gave me the money and a decent tip and told me I could drive anywhere I wanted, but I had to have her back to that address in three hours. I asked if anyone else was going to join her on the journey, and she turned sideways and this little skinny guy was standing just behind her. I looked at him and thought, *Oh man, good luck, fella!*

At the back of this particular limo, you could pull the back off and see outside. I did that for them, and they were probably the quietest clients I have ever had. They were way in the back enjoying themselves while I just drove them around wherever they wanted to go. Most of the time, they told me it didn't matter and just to drive anywhere; I even stopped to get a bite to eat at a drive-in during the journey. I gave them an extra ten minutes, which is something I always did to make sure you got your money's worth, and then I pulled back up at the pick-up address, dropped them off, and said, "Thank you very much. You have been a delight. I hope to see you again one day." Customer service is always a key thing for me, and if you are good to me, I will always be good to you and do all that I can to make sure your time with me is memorable.

I have driven movie stars, rock bands, CEOs, broadcast journalists, NFL players, and supermodels over the years. I once drove a New Orleans senator on a wine tour, and we had an amazing time. We got on so well that by the end we even hugged when we said farewell. I have had the pleasure of driving for people from all over the world. I often get jobs that involve people from England, and we usually have a great time.

People from the UK often understand me really well because they have all read about the history of San Francisco. Honestly, I have picked up kids from the UK who knew more about the city than I did; they even taught me new things! They have read all about the different parts of the city and know all the places they want to visit and a lot about the history of those locations. At the other end of the scale, I have also worked for people who are a similar age to me, and they also seemed to know a lot about the city and we had an equally great time. It is, more often than not, the people you drive around that make this type of work so enjoyable.

I occasionally took this one group of people to Las Vegas, and they always had sex the whole way; on the floors, on the seats, all over the place. They were part of a swinger's club, and they certainly swung during these trips. During one journey to Vegas, it was all going on back there, and I had to pull over on the side of the freeway and join in; there was no way I could concentrate on my driving with all that going on behind me. I asked if I could join and who fancied it, and one lady simply put her hand up and off we went. They often stopped in Vegas overnight and then I drove them back the next day. I did that a few times, and it was always an interesting adventure.

Unfortunately, on the other side of the coin, as is the case in so many walks of life, there are always the idiots and passengers who you just can't deal with. I was out on the bus one afternoon and had this group of guys on board. They acted like they were corporate big shots and behaved like real assholes; they kicked the poles, knocked things over, and fought like kids. I asked them to calm down and told them they couldn't fight on the bus and continue doing the things they were doing. I asked them politely and told them I didn't want to have to throw them off the bus for poor behavior while I was at the wheel. That is the sort of thing that can lead to accidents.

Straightaway, a few of the mouthier ones started to shout at me, "Oh right, sure, you can't throw all thirty-seven of us off!" I immediately pulled over on the side of Highway 101, stopped right there, pulled out the machete I kept under the seat for protection, and said, "No, I can't throw you all off and no, I can't kill all of you, but I am going to get at least three or four of you motherfuckers … so who's it gonna be!?" They all got off the bus nice and quiet, and I drove off and left them on the side of the 101 freeway, still in their tuxedos.

Another time I had a group from Oakland, and I make no bones about it, I always made them pay up-front due to the reputation of that city. They also pushed things too far, threatened to do this to me and that to me. I would tell them everything was all cool and to calm down. As soon as they got out and went to a bar, I drove out of there as quickly as I could, and they never saw me again. Of course, they phoned up the company, and I told the boss what they had said and done and then I firmly told him, "Ah fuck them, there is no way I am going back to get them after what they have said and done!"

Another less-than-pleasant instance happened on Van Ness Avenue. It was prom time, and to be honest, I know it's a busy time for limo drivers, but I always avoid those types of jobs if I can. The kids on this particular occasion wanted a pickup and drop-off, a type of job that the company I worked for offered all the time. It's a cheaper rate and is a pickup and a drop-off and that is it.

I tried to be as nice as I could to this group of teenagers. They wanted to stop here and then stop there, and I did it for them; I genuinely wanted them to have a good time. However, they wanted to stop off a third or fourth time somewhere else, so I had to say to them, "I am sorry. I can't, because you are already over your time and I have done a couple of stops for you already, which I am not supposed to do. I have to get you back now." Suddenly, one of the kids slapped me hard in the back of the head and told me to just do what they had asked.

I slammed on the brakes and threw the limo in park. All of them in the back bounced up in the air and by the time they had landed I had charged in through the back door. I trampled through the other passengers and grabbed that little shit. I then dragged him through his friends and out of the limo. I do not mind telling you I gave that ungrateful bastard quite a beating. If it wasn't for one of the girls near the back door who begged me not to kill him, I suspect I would have done that boy some serious harm! It has rarely happened during my time as a limo driver but that is one instance where I seriously lost it with someone.

There was another time when I came close to it. Just before you get to the Golden Gate Bridge, right there on the marina where you see all those boats, there is the St. Francis Yacht Club. I once had a booking to collect some people from there for a three-hour trip in my limo. When I got there, a couple of people jumped in the back and then this guy ran over and jumped in the car with them. He was a total idiot and tried to say to me, "Hey driver, I want you to go here. I want you to go there." He was really obnoxious and you could tell the couple was not impressed, so I turned around and said, "Now, let me tell you one thing right now. I already don't like your ass, because you're rich, you feel entitled, and because of the way you just spoke to me. If you say another fucking word to me again like that, I am going to come back there and kick your ass! Do you understand me clearly?" He jumped out of the car in seconds, and the other people told me they were glad about it as they didn't like him very much themselves. We took off, and they had a great time for the rest of the booking.

People just get to me sometimes. I don't consider myself a chauffeur, because chauffeurs know how to talk and get around that sort of thing; I consider myself a driver. I am the first to admit that I do have a bit of an attitude problem sometimes, but I think that comes from where I grew up and the life that I have led. Make no mistake; I can get right back on you as quickly as you like, be it verbally or physically if the situation calls for it. The problem is that sometimes you get these entitled pricks or these little rich kids who think they can do whatever they want and just get away with it. They think because they have money, that gives them the right to say and do whatever they want, to treat people in any way they want, and just get away with it because of where they come from!

Nowadays, people are not used to a proper ass kicking. My friends and I have talked about this often over the last twenty-odd years: "They never had a good ass kicking and that is why they behave the way they do!"

Hollywood Hustle

Players from the Raiders were not the only famous people I have driven around. Toward the end of the nineties, I worked for a year and a half on the TV show *Nash Bridges* with Don Johnson. It was a program based around a special unit in the San Francisco Police Department. I was even in one of the limos during an actual scene. A car tried to get in between me and the cameras while we drove along Broadway in Oakland. I was in my limo, and I swooped ahead of him and cut in behind the camera again. When it was over, Don Johnson said to me, "You know what? That was some pretty fancy driving!" It meant a lot to me to hear that, so I said, "You know what? Let's flip this thing."

I always wanted to flip a limo in a movie because they say it can't be done easily. He wasn't up for that and said, "Oh no, you do that on your own time." I came up with more ideas like, "If we put it up on two wheels, me and you on two wheels, with the cameras on us ..." Sadly, he still didn't go for the idea and told me to do stuff like that on my own time. After that, he hired me to drive his kids to places like Great America. I think that scene broke the ice with Don and myself because I only drove his crew around in the limo bus prior to that. I also drove Johnny Mathis around for his fiftieth anniversary when he appeared on KQED-FM. I drove him through the city. He grew up in San Francisco, so it was a very interesting tour with him. He actually grew up around Washington High School and that is where my wife went to school. We had a really good conversation because his father was like me. He told me his father came from Texas and he knew how to cook Creole food. We had a real one-on-one conversation. It was one of my favorite jobs as a driver.

I also drove Barbara Walters and I told her, "Barbara, I can die and go to heaven now," and she asked me why. I replied, "Because I have met Barbara Walters." She smiled and said that I was so sweet.

Another famous lady who has been in my limo is Tyra Banks. It happened about three or four years ago when I drove up to the Intercontinental Hotel on Howard Street. I saw this beautiful woman who looked like a model, and she was just walking around outside the front of the hotel. I asked one of my friends who worked there, "Who is that? Do you know who that is?" It was nothing more than simple curiosity at the time.

He told me it was Tyra Banks, and when I asked him what she was doing standing outside the hotel, he said, "She is waiting on her Uber." I replied straightaway, "Oh no, she ain't riding in no Uber, not as long as I am here!" I drove up to her and told her to get in the limo. She asked if I was her car, and I was honest and said to her, "No, but I am here to take you to the airport." When she said to me that she had paid for an Uber, I explained that the ride was free. There was no way I was going to let someone like Tyra Banks ride in an Uber when I was there to drive her in a limo.

She took me up on the offer and as we drove to the airport along the freeway, I couldn't help but ask, "How long are those legs anyway?" She leaned back and put them up on my arm rest, and before I knew it, I had my arm and elbow around her legs; I made sure I didn't touch them with my hands. I held them the whole way to the airport, and when we got to her terminal, I still had ahold of them. She said, "Can I have my legs back?" I quickly moved my arms, but I made a point of saying that I was going to tell everyone that Tyra Banks told me to give her back her legs.

She said, "You are something else." I told her I was more than that. She asked how much she owed me, and I told her it was free, but she insisted on paying for the ride. Meeting Tyra Banks was one of those highly unexpected yet absolutely delightful things that happen when you are a limo driver and find yourself in the right place at the right time.

That is a little insight into my life as a limo driver. I still have my limo business and continue to work as a driver to this very day. It's an interesting and varied job, and you never know what each trip and each customer is going to bring to your day. As I look back over the last thirty years, it's a decision I am very glad that I made back in the early nineties, and it's a job that I still thoroughly enjoy.

CHAPTER 8

The Present Day and My Foundation

There is not much I can say about the last ten years. They have been fairly quiet and not much has happened. I intend to continue working in the limo business for as long as I can, even if I do work less regularly than I used to. In fact, just the other day I drove some clients to a birthday party at a steak house located in Santana Row, San Jose. That is a beautiful-looking area, kind of ritzy. They kindly bought me dinner, and it was a nice evening all around.

I suppose we all calm down as we get older, although that doesn't mean I am ready to retire with a pipe and slippers just yet. It just means I have a bit more time to think about what I want to do with my remaining years. Looking forward, there is something that I started a few years ago, and it's something that is very special to me and very close to my heart.

A few years ago, I started my own nonprofit foundation, and the eventual aim is to provide something like a residential camp/boarding school homeless children, deprived children, and children from broken homes. It has been an ongoing thing for about six years now, and it has yet to pan out in the way that I would have hoped. Sadly, quite often when you have a good idea to help people, you struggle to get people's attention, but when you have a crooked idea to steal from people, then suddenly you seem to be able to get people involved.

My whole idea is to break the chain of kids living the same rough life that their parents went through, assuming they even have parents. You constantly hear these stories about children living this rough life, even if both their parents are still involved or around. Their parents can't find any work, and even if they can sometimes get a job, it's often a low-paid position with no prospects and they still live a miserable existence. Often, the kid involved in this situation is a very bright child; if they had a chance in life, they could be somebody. I want to build something like a residential camp that acts as a boarding school. It would be a similar type of boarding school to the one that richer kids get sent to by their parents so they get a good education. The foundation is something I've long wanted to get off the ground but haven't quite yet made headway.

Personally, I think you have to break the chain. The story flows from one poor kid to the next generation of poor kids and then to the next generation of poor kids, and on and on it goes. If you look at any successful family, maybe even just look at our presidential families like the Kennedys or the Bush family, they all continued in a similarly successful life to that of their parents.

You will often see that the child of a doctor or a lawyer goes on to be a doctor or a lawyer, and even if they choose a different career path, they are still successful. There is occasionally one person that becomes the black sheep in a successful family but that is a rarity rather than the rule, and the same goes for the poorer families. Yes, the exception to the rule does break the cycle. You could even count me as one of them, but again, that is a rarity rather than a regular occurrence.

My father was a working man and I became a working man. I think it goes in an ever-revolving circle. As a kid, you grow up and see your parents constantly struggling, and you just think to yourself, *That is just the way it is*, even though you see all the rich people around you. Kids from tough backgrounds quickly end up just saying, "That is just the way things are. I guess I will end up in a minimum wage job as well if I am lucky."

I want to build a boarding school/camp-like place for kids but not one where kids go for a couple of weeks during the summer. I am not talking about the sort of camp where kids can ride horses, swim in lakes, and spend a few weeks away from their parents. The type of camp I have in mind would be about living a different way of life and not trying new things for a few weeks in the summer.

The kids would live on the premises, and there would be things like a wood shop, a mechanic shop, a computer shop. The kid would grow up there and get the education they need to be able to get on in life. I suppose you could say it is more like something from the film *Major Payne* than the

Crystal Lake summer camp in a film like *Friday the 13th*. In the former, most of the kids paid to go there, but they had a little program for the underprivileged kids.

The school I have in mind would be entirely for that sort of child. It would be there to offer them education in all sorts of different professions and, in doing so, put them into a different frame of mind where they feel they can achieve more than they otherwise could. Once they reach a certain age, the long-term plan would be to help them to get into college straight after they graduate from the boarding school. It would eventually be a full program where the kid can go from deprived or homeless to a fully educated young adult. Thanks to all the training and education, they can then go on to a decent life.

Nowadays, all these organizations place the children—and sometimes the parents and the children—in homes. What good does that do? You place the parents and kids in a home, and they still grow up in poverty. The cycle continues. When the kids get older, they repeat the same path and again that family or their children then get placed in a home. It's a vicious circle. I want to smash that circle. It might sound harsh to say it, but forget the parents, focus on the kids; get them out of that cycle and the homelessness will, for the most part, die out. I would love to say this sort of idea could end homelessness or at least solve a large percentage of it. I know as a society we will never be able to eradicate it completely, but we can at least try to break it by changing the kids' lives so they go on to become somebody. Who knows? Maybe the first generation of kids through the foundation will help the next generation and so on. I know that any kid who goes through the foundation and school will be worried about their parents, especially if their parents are struggling, but they can help them in the workshop by building things for them. They can build a table, benches, maybe even beds. It's a twofold bonus: the child learns a trade and helps their parents at the same time. As for the parents, there can be parent's day when they come out and see the progress their kid has made and also all the potential they have available to them.

The reason I made it a nonprofit is because when I die and go away, the business will continue with my ideals. If someone takes over the foundation, they have to continue with my idea of what I wanted it to be. It is not like a regular business or company, where you have to make a profit and keep shareholders happy. Of course, you have to pay wages to the teachers and the people who run the camp, but the idea is that as much money as possible is returned to the foundation so it can help the next generation of kids.

My idea goes further than just a school or a camp. The idea is that it would be like a ranch where a lot of the food is raised or grown on site. It could become a self-sufficient entity. You could grow fruits and vegetables, have livestock for meat and milk, chickens for eggs, etc. That way the kids not only learn about a profession or trade (woodwork, mechanics, and suchlike) but they also learn how to live off the land, cook all the things that are grown on the ranch, and how to breed or look after animals. It would give them a much better appreciation of life rather than simply buying food in bulk from somewhere like Costco. My wife and I have always loved children, and to see the foundation come to life and help give kids a better life would be something that I would cherish.

I grew up a certain way, and I liked what I was doing. As I look back, it might not have been the right way and it might not be the way I would have wanted my kids to grow up, but it was good for me. However, there was one all-important aspect that was at the center of everything I did—whether I was a kid, a teenager, or a grown man—and it's something that sadly too many people either forget or ignore.

No matter what the job or situation, I was always willing, and always expected, to work hard to earn the money I needed to provide all the things I wanted and later to provide for my family. Those options, whether they were right or wrong, are not even available now (or not in a way that has any long-term benefit). Therefore, if I can give back to the community and provide a new pathway for kids, that is what I want to do.

That is the legacy that I want to leave, not only to offer a route for struggling kids but to show them what someone can achieve if they are willing to work hard, even a hustler like me.

CHAPTER 9

The Last Word

I was involved in a lot of different things as a kid growing up. Sometimes you don't know where your place is in life. You try this and you try that. I think that is where I was during the early days. In the end, I became a family man with a wife and kids. I am more than happy that I got married and had kids, and if I were to do it all over again, I would still make that decision, but maybe I should have stayed in the game, maybe I should have kept working with all the girls, and maybe I should have continued that life as well.

I thought about it a lot at the time, but as I watched my kids get older and they started to grow up, I told myself that the best decision for them would be to move out of the city and get a house in a nicer area. If I am honest with myself, I know that I would have wondered the same thing in reverse had I stayed in that style of life. My kids would have had a different upbringing, and there is no doubt about that, and I would not have wanted them to be around that sort of life.

You are always taking chances, and your luck will run out in the end. Even though I had the police on my side, having saved that officer's life, and I had an advantage because of that, it was an advantage that would only have helped me so far. There would always have been officers who wouldn't care about that.

As I look back, I had all the business I could handle. Of course, I could have done more. I could have probably gotten more and been bigger, but there was no way in the world I would have wanted to be a drug lord or something like that. When you get that big, you get noticed, no matter what good you have done elsewhere. I wanted to be just how I was, and just like I ended up: a hustler, a host of great parties, and a damn good limo driver.

My whole life was one big hustle and it's been one hell of a ride. The people I met became my family. We were a family of life that enjoyed living; we loved to dress in nice clothes and drive great cars. We partied as hard as anyone around at that time, and we were more or less movie stars without being actual movie stars.

Looking back over all these memories as I wrote this book, I am thankful to have grown up and lived during the time that I did. As I said at the start, many people think I have lived an amazing life and many people have told me they wished they had lived my life; now you know my story as well.

The only thing left for me to say is that having revisited all these crazy moments. I am truly blessed to have lived through such an interesting time. San Francisco will never be the same again, and I am extremely fortunate to have lived there and experienced it during its heyday. I suppose I should also be grateful to have lived to tell this tale—the story of sex and drugs and a man who was born and raised to be a hustler in San Francisco during the good old days.

Made in the USA
Columbia, SC
01 May 2025